Celebrate Freedom

Celebrate Freedom

Our country has three important papers. These are the Declaration of Independence, the Constitution, and the Bill of Rights. Read about what these three papers say.

Declaration of Independence, 1776

We want to be free from England. We think all people should be free and equal.

- **Why do you think it is important to be free?**

Constitution of the United States of America, 1789

We want to make a better country. We need laws that will be fair to everyone.

- **What kind of laws do we need?**

Bill of Rights, 1791

We are making a list of ten freedoms for all Americans. Two of them are:

- freedom to talk about our ideas
- freedom to pray as we wish

- **Why do you think these freedoms are important?**

Materials:
- Pencil
- Crayons
- Tracing Paper

Color the First American Flag

Long ago our country had only 13 states. Our first flag had only 13 stars.

Today our country has 50 states, so our flag has 50 stars.

1. Trace the drawing of our first flag.

2. Color your flag red, white, and blue as shown.

Make a Freedom Poster

The Bill of Rights lists different freedoms. All Americans share these freedoms.

1. Draw a picture that shows a freedom that you have.
2. Label your poster.

Freedom to Talk About Our Ideas

Celebrate Freedom

The Pledge of Allegiance

I pledge allegiance to the flag of the United States of America and to the Republic for which it stands, one Nation under God, indivisible, with liberty and justice for all.

The National Anthem

Oh, say, can you see, by the dawn's early light,
What so proudly we hailed at the twilight's last gleaming?
Whose broad stripes and bright stars,
Thro' the perilous fight, O'er the ramparts
We watched, were so gallantly streaming?
And the rockets' red glare, the bombs bursting in air,
Gave proof through the night that our flag was still there.
Oh, say, does that Star-Spangled Banner yet wave
O'er the land of the free and the home of the brave?

A7

Great Americans

Americans love the United States. They love our country's freedom. Read what two great Americans said about freedom.

John Adams

The second President of the United States wanted to keep our country strong.
"Swim or sink, live or die . . . I am with my country."

Rosa Parks

Rosa worked to make sure that African Americans were treated fairly.

"I wanted freedom .... It did not matter how much I needed to work [for it]."

Geography

RUSSIA

PACIFIC OCEAN

Alaska

CANADA

Bering Sea

Gulf of Alaska

PACIFIC OCEAN

American Life in the Past

National parks can show you how Americans lived long ago. Just like today, American families built homes. Children learned at school. Families worked and played together.

⭐ **Where can you learn about Americans long ago?**

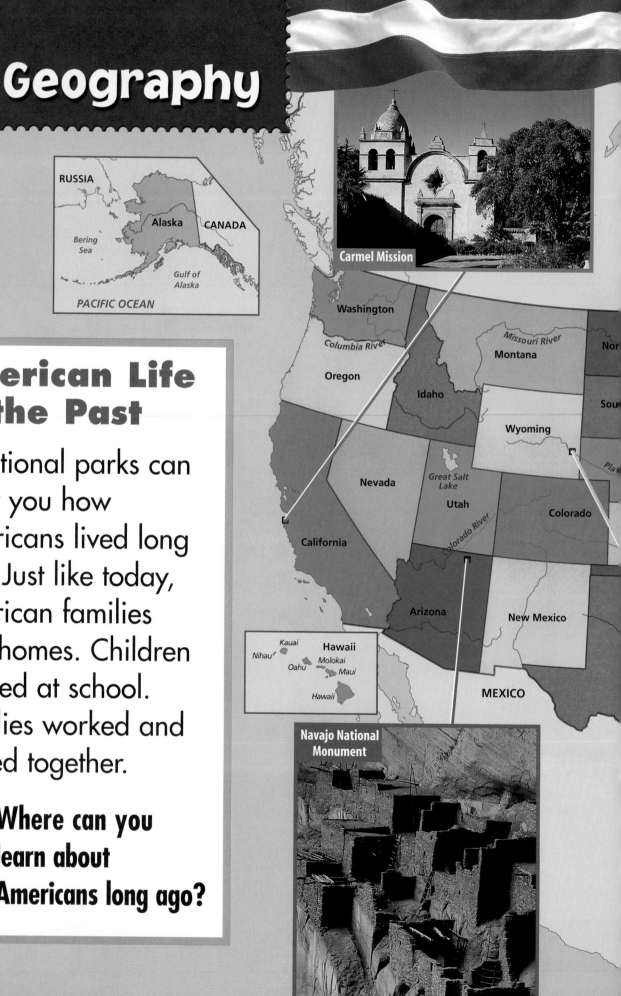

Carmel Mission

Washington

Columbia River

Oregon

Idaho

Montana

Missouri River

Nor

Wyoming

Sou

Nevada

Great Salt Lake

Utah

Colorado

Pla

California

Colorado River

Arizona

New Mexico

Kauai

Hawaii

Nihau

Oahu

Molokai

Maui

Hawaii

MEXICO

Navajo National Monument

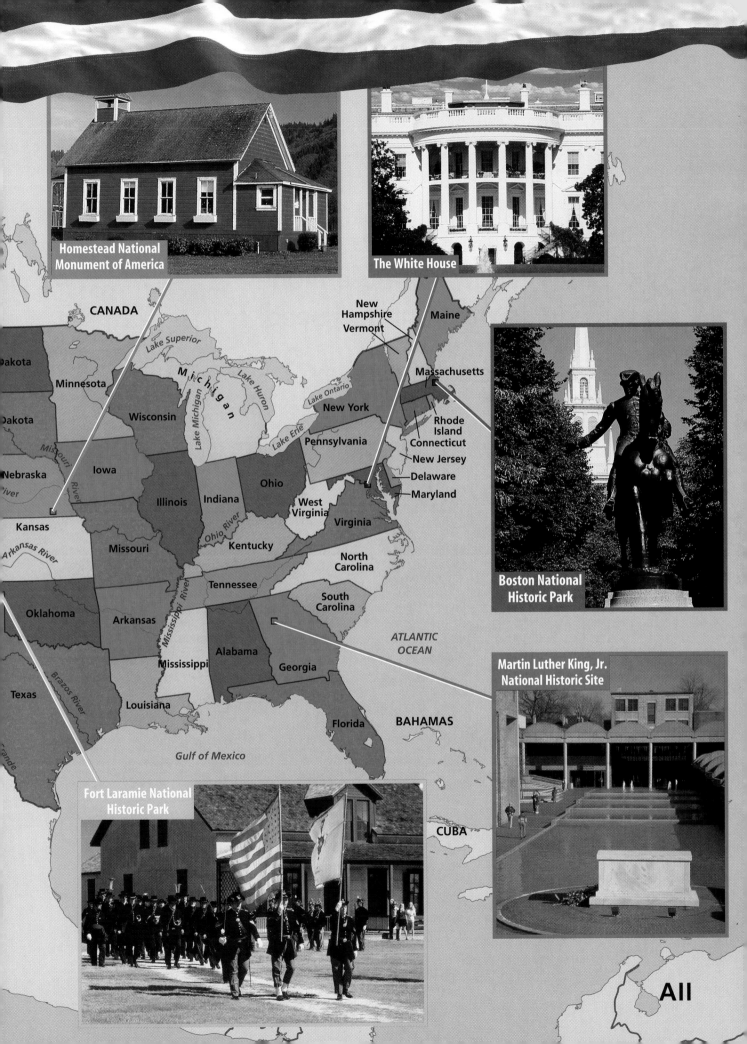

Homestead National
Monument of America

The White House

Boston National
Historic Park

Martin Luther King, Jr.
National Historic Site

Fort Laramie National
Historic Park

CANADA

Lake Superior

Michigan

Lake Huron

Lake Michigan

Lake Ontario

Lake Erie

Dakota

Minnesota

Dakota

Wisconsin

Missouri River

Nebraska

Iowa

Illinois

Indiana

Ohio

Pennsylvania

New York

New
Hampshire
Vermont

Maine

Massachusetts

Rhode
Island
Connecticut
New Jersey
Delaware
Maryland

Kansas

Arkansas River

Missouri

Ohio River

Kentucky

West
Virginia

Virginia

North
Carolina

Oklahoma

Arkansas

Tennessee

South
Carolina

ATLANTIC
OCEAN

Texas

Brazos River

Mississippi

Mississippi River

Alabama

Georgia

Louisiana

Florida

BAHAMAS

Gulf of Mexico

CUBA

All

Economics

Money

Our government makes coins and paper money. We use money to buy things we want and need.

✓ **What do we do with money?**

Government

Our Leaders

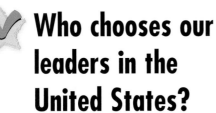

Americans who are at least 18 years old choose our leaders. Some leaders work in Washington, D.C. They work to help people and make laws.

✓ **Who chooses our leaders in the United States?**

Citizenship

Community Helpers

Many people help us to stay safe. Firefighters rescue people. They put out fires. Firefighters want you to be safe if there is a fire.

★ **What do firefighters do?**

Culture

Sports

Culture means the ways people do things. In our country, people skate, play soccer, and other sports.

 What is culture?

Science, Technology, and Society

Inventors

Inventors are people who make things that have never been made before. The Wright Brothers invented the first plane.

What do inventors do?

Orville and Wilbur Wright

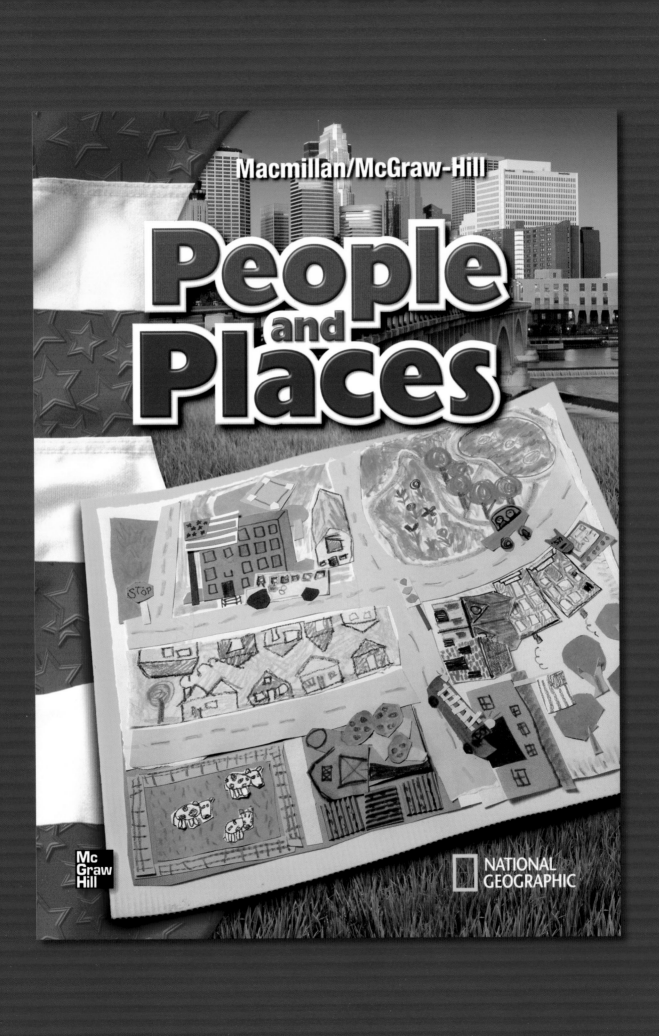

About the Cover: A view of downtown Minneapolis, Minnesota, rising above the Mississippi River appears on the cover. In the foreground, there is a community map made by a child.

Macmillan/McGraw-Hill

People and Places

James A. Banks

Richard G. Boehm

Kevin P. Colleary

Gloria Contreras

A. Lin Goodwin

Mary A. McFarland

Walter C. Parker

NATIONAL GEOGRAPHIC

Macmillan
McGraw-Hill
New York

PROGRAM AUTHORS

Dr. James A. Banks
Russell F. Stark University Professor and Director of the Center for Multicultural Education
University of Washington
Seattle, Washington

Dr. Richard G. Boehm
Jesse H. Jones Distinguished Chair in Geographic Education and Director, The Gilbert M. Grosvenor Center for Geographic Education
Southwest Texas State University
San Marcos, Texas

Dr. Kevin P. Colleary
Curriculum and Teaching Department
Hunter College
City University of New York
New York, New York

Dr. Gloria Contreras
Professor of Education
University of North Texas
Denton, Texas

Dr. A. Lin Goodwin
Associate Professor of Education
Department of Curriculum and Teaching
Teachers College
Columbia University
New York, New York

Dr. Mary A. McFarland
Social Studies Educational Consultant, K-12
St. Louis, Missouri

Dr. Walter C. Parker
Professor of Education and Chair of Social Studies Education
University of Washington
Seattle, Washington

NATIONAL GEOGRAPHIC
Washington, D.C.

HISTORIANS/SCHOLARS

Dr. Joyce Appleby
Professor of History
University of California, Los Angeles
Los Angeles, California

Dr. Alan Brinkley
Professor of American History
Columbia University
New York, New York

Dr. Nancy Cott
Stanley Woodward Professor of History and American Studies
Yale University
New Haven, Connecticut

Dr. James McPherson
George Henry Davis Professor of American History
Princeton University
Princeton, New Jersey

Dr. Donald A. Ritchie
Associate Historian of the United States Senate Historical Office
Washington, D.C.

PROGRAM CONSULTANTS

Betty Ruth Baker, M.Ed
Assistant Professor of Curriculum and Instruction
Early Childhood Specialist
School of Education
Baylor University
Waco, Texas

Dr. Randolph B. Campbell
Regents' Professor of History
University of North Texas
Denton, Texas

Dr. Steven Cobb
Director, Center for Economic Education
Chair, Department of Economics
University of North Texas
Denton, Texas

Frank de Varona, Ed.S.
Visiting Associate Professor
Florida International University
Miami, Florida

Dr. John L. Esposito
Professor of Religion and International Affairs, and Director of the Center for Christian-Muslim Understanding
Georgetown University
Washington, D.C.

READING INSTRUCTION CONSULTANTS

M. Frankie Dungan, M.Ed.
Reading/Language Arts Consultant, K–6
Mansfield, Texas

Antonio A. Fierro
Program Director for the Texas Reading Initiative, Region 19
El Paso, Texas

Carol Ritchey, M.Ed.
Reading Specialist
Tarver Rendon Elementary School
Burleson, Texas

Dr. William H. Rupley
Professor of Reading Education
Distinguished Research Fellow
Department of Teaching, Learning and Culture
College of Education
Texas A&M University
College Station, Texas

GRADE LEVEL CONSULTANTS

Aimee Bailey
First Grade Teacher
Woodlake Elementary School
San Antonio, Texas

Theresa Barnett
First Grade Teacher
Martin Weiss Elementary School
Dallas, Texas

Ruby Finney
First Grade Teacher
Blanton Elementary School
Carrollton, Texas

Catheline Jones
First Grade Teacher
Gateway Elementary School
St. Louis, Missouri

Betty Kinner
Staff Development Resource Teacher
Seminole County Public Schools
Sanford, Florida

Kristine Klein
First Grade Teacher
Red Bug Elementary School
Casselberry, Florida

Layne Pethick
Special Education Teacher
H. K. Williams Elementary School
San Antonio, Texas

Ana Tinajero
First Grade Teacher
Ramona Elementary School
El Paso, Texas

Karen Waldstein
Social Studies Curriculum Resource Specialist, K–8
Framingham Public Schools
Framingham, Massachusetts

Patricia Walshe
First Grade Teacher
Desert Hills Elementary School
El Paso, Texas

CONTRIBUTING WRITERS

Dinah Zike
Comfort, Texas

Becky Manfredini
Calabasas, California

Linda Scher
Raleigh, North Carolina

learning through listening

Students with print disabilities may be eligible to obtain an accessible, audio version of the pupil edition of this textbook. Please call Recording for the Blind & Dyslexic at 1-800-221-4792 for complete information.

Acknowledgments

The publisher gratefully acknowledges permission to reprint the following copyrighted material:

"Pride" and "Orgullo" from **Gathering the Sun** by Alma Flor Ada. Copyright © 1997 by Alma Flor Ada. Lothrop, Lee & Shephard Books, a division of William Morrrow and Company, Inc. All rights reserved. Used by permission. From **Edison's Electric Light: Biography of an Invention** by Robert Friedel & Paul Israel with Bernard S. Finn. Copyright © 1986 by Rutgers, The State University. Used by permission. From "Big Beautiful Planet," adapted by Raffi & Louise Dain Cullen. Copyright © 1976 Homeland Publishing, a division of Troubadour Records Ltd. All rights reserved. From **Always, Rachel: The Letters of Rachel Carson and Dorothy Freeman, 1952–1964.** Copyright © 1994 Beacon Press. Used by permission.

(continued on page R20)

Macmillan/McGraw-Hill
A Division of The **McGraw·Hill** Companies

Printed in the United States of America

ISBN 0-02-149262-X

5 6 7 8 9 110/043 06 05 04 03

Contents

SOCIAL STUDIES HANDBOOK

NATIONAL GEOGRAPHIC

The Eight Strands of Social Studies H1

Reading Social Studies H3

The Elements of Geography H7

    Understanding Geography Skills H9

Unit 1

📖 **Literature** "Hooray for Saturday!" 2

All About Families 8

The Big Idea What is a Family? 10

Words To Know About Families 12

Lesson 1 Many Families 14

Lesson 2 Families Celebrate 18

Celebrate "Pride" by Alma Flor Ada 22

Lesson 3 Where Families Live 24

NATIONAL GEOGRAPHIC

◉ Geography Skills Using Addresses 28

Lesson 4 Family Rules 30

◉ Reading and Thinking Skills Problem Solving 34

Lesson 5 Families on the Move 36

◉ Study Skills Using Charts 40

Lesson 6 Families and Change 42

Biography Thomas Edison 46

★ Citizenship Helping Kids Have Fun 48

The World Around Us A Family Celebrating in Kenya 50

UNIT 1 Review 52

Unit 2

Literature "The Legend of Johnny Appleseed" . . . 56

Where We Live 60

The Big Idea What is Geography? 62

Words To Know About Geography 64

Lesson 1 We Live in Communities 66

NATIONAL GEOGRAPHIC

◉ **Geography Skills** Using Pictures and Maps 72

Lesson 2 Our Country 74

◉ **Reading and Thinking Skills** Sorting into Groups 76

Lesson 3 Our World 78

Celebrate "Big Beautiful Planet" by Raffi 84

Lesson 4 Water and Land 86

NATIONAL GEOGRAPHIC

◉ **Geography Skills** Using Map Keys 90

Lesson 5 What is Weather? 92

Lesson 6 Caring for Our Natural Resources 96

Biography Rachel Carson 102

★ **Citizenship** Keeping Our World Clean 104

The World Around Us Geography in Switzerland 106

UNIT 2 Review 108

Unit 3

Literature "A Good Helper" 112

Good Citizens 118

The Big Idea What Makes a Good Citizen? 120

Words To Know About Citizenship 122

Lesson 1 People Get Along 124

NATIONAL GEOGRAPHIC

◉ **Geography Skills** Using Directions 128

Lesson 2 People Follow Laws 130

Lesson 3 What is a Leader? 132

Biography Mary McLeod Bethune 136

★ **Citizenship** Getting Along at School 138

Lesson 4 Votes Count! 140

Lesson 5 Our Symbols and Pledge 142

● **Study Skills** Using the Calendar 150

Lesson 6 Good Citizens 152

Celebrate "My Country, 'Tis of Thee" 158

The World Around Us First Graders in Japan 160

UNIT 3 Review 162

Unit 4

📖 **Literature** "The Ant and the Grasshopper" 166

All Kinds Of Jobs 170

The Big Idea What is Work? 172

Words To Know About Economics 174

Lesson 1 Needs and Wants 176

Lesson 2 Work and Jobs 180

Celebrate Paintings by William Gropper 184

Lesson 3 Goods and Services 186

● **Study Skills** Using Picture Graphs 190

Lesson 4 Getting Goods and Services 192

Biography Cesar Chavez 196

★ **Citizenship** Being Fair 198

Lesson 5 New Tools at Work 200

● **Reading and Thinking Skills** Putting Things in Order . . . 204

Lesson 6 People with Great Ideas 206

The World Around Us Jobs in Brazil 210

UNIT 4 Review 212

Unit 5

📖 **Literature** "My Grandma and Me" 216

Americans Long Ago 220

The Big Idea What is History? 222

Words To Know About History 224

Lesson 1 Native Americans Then and Now 226

◉ **Study Skills** Using Time Lines 232

Lesson 2 New People Come to America 234

Lesson 3 George Washington 240

Lesson 4 Sacajawea 244

Biography Sam Houston 246

Lesson 5 Abraham Lincoln 248

Lesson 6 Susan B. Anthony 252

◉ **Reading and Thinking Skills** Finding the Main Idea . 256

Celebrate "Veterans Day with Grandpa" by Bobbi Katz . 258

Lesson 7 Martin Luther King, Jr. 260

⭐ **Citizenship** Ask a Friend 264

The World Around Us A Hero from Mexico 266

UNIT 5 Review 268

Celebrate Holidays 272

REFERENCE SECTION

Atlas . . . . R2   Picture Glossary R8
Dictionary of Geographic Words . . . . . R6   Index R18

FEATURES

Skills

◉ **Reading and Thinking Skills**
Problem Solving 34
Sorting into Groups 76
Putting Things in Order 204
Finding the Main Idea 256

◉ **Geography Skills**   NATIONAL GEOGRAPHIC
Using Addresses 28
Using Pictures and Maps 72
Using Map Keys 90
Using Directions 128

◉ Study Skills
Using Charts 40
Using the Calendar 150
Using Picture Graphs 190
Using Time Lines. 232

✪ Citizenship
Being a Good Citizen
Helping Kids Have Fun 48
Getting Along at School 138
Ask a Friend 264

Making Decisions
Keeping Our World Clean 104
Being Fair. 198

Biography
Thomas Edison 46
Rachel Carson 102
Mary McLeod Bethune 136

Cesar Chavez 196
Sam Houston 246

Celebrate
"Pride" by Alma Flor Ada. 22
"Big Beautiful Planet" by Raffi 84
"My Country, 'Tis of Thee" music
   by Henry Carey, words by Samuel
   F. Smith. 158
Paintings by William Gropper 184
"Veterans Day with Grandpa" by
   Bobbi Katz 258

In Their Own Words:
Primary Sources
Thomas Edison 47
Rachel Carson 103
Nathan Hale 152
Ellen Ochoa. 209
Martin Luther King, Jr. 262

CHARTS AND GRAPHS

Chart • Transportation to Mike's
   Favorite Places. 40
Chart • Ways to Send Messages. 45
Chart • Ways to Help at Home. 53
Chart • Weather. 93
Chart • Classroom Rules 127
Calendar • July. 151

Calendar • November 164
Picture Graph • Painting the House. . . 191
Picture Graph • Jill's Jobs. 195
Picture Graph • Shoes Sold in
   Three Days 213
Time Line • Rosa's Time Line 232
Time Line • Matt's Time Line 269

MAPS

Playground H10
Globe. H12
Pittsburgh, Pennsylvania 49
Kenya. 51
Chicago, Illinois 67
Clovis, California. 69
Lewisburg, West Virginia 71
Ajay's Community. 73
The United States of America 74
The United States and Its Neighbors . . 79
The World. 80
Where You Live 82
A Country Community. 91
Texas and Washington. 93
Kentucky's Resources 99
Switzerland 107

My Town 109
Classroom 129
Oakland, California 139
Japan 161
School 163
Brazil 211
New Mexico 229
Florida 231
Columbus Sails West. 235
Santa Fe, New Mexico 237
The Pilgrims' Trip 239
Morrisville, North Carolina 265
Mexico 267
The United States. R2
The World. R4

Social Studies Handbook

The Eight Strands of Social Studies

There are many parts to social studies. Look at the pictures to learn more.

History

- The story of the past

Economics

- Meeting our needs and wants

Geography

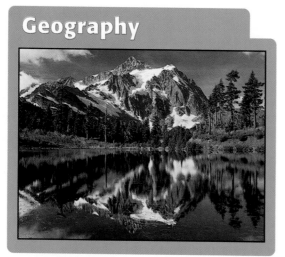

- People and places on Earth

Government

- Leaders and laws

Citizenship

- Rules and responsibilities

Culture

- The way of life shared by a group of people

Science, Technology, and Society

- New ideas and tools changing the way people live

Social Studies Skills

- Reading, thinking, and studying

Thinking About Reading

Knowing how to use your book is important. Here are three steps you can use to become a good social studies reader.

1 **Look Through the Lesson.** Read the titles. Look at the pictures and maps. What is the lesson about?

2 **Ask Questions While You Read.** Ask yourself questions like, "Why is this important?"

3 **Think.** Think about what you have read. What did you learn?

Different Kinds of Land

① **Look.**
The title and pictures tell me this lesson is about land.

Flat land is called a **plain**. The state of Iowa is part of a big plain. This plain is the biggest in our country.

② **Ask.**
Ask yourself, "Why is it important to know about land?"

A **hill** is land higher than the land around it. There are many hills in the state of Idaho.

③ **Think.**
Think about what you learned about land.

Plain

Hill

H4

Using Pictures

Looking at pictures will help you understand what you read.

Look at this picture. Ask yourself these questions:

- What does the picture show?

- Does the picture have a label? What does it tell me?

Look at the chart below. It tells you about the picture.

crossing guard

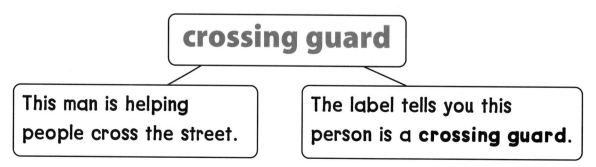

crossing guard

This man is helping people cross the street.

The label tells you this person is a **crossing guard**.

Look at the picture below. What does it show? Copy the chart under the picture. Fill in what the picture shows.

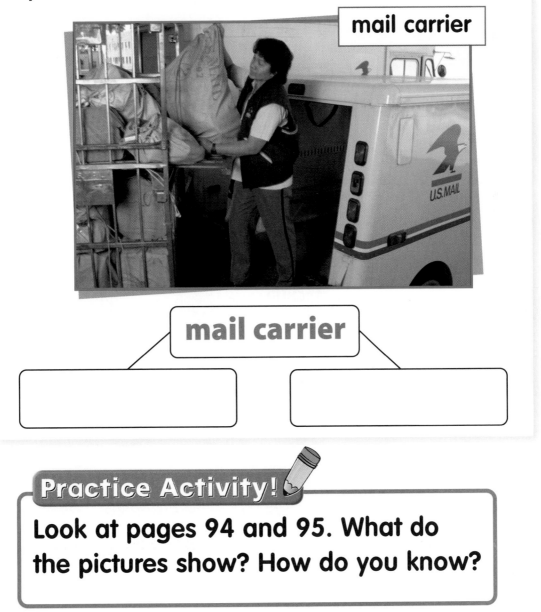

mail carrier

mail carrier

Practice Activity!

Look at pages 94 and 95. What do the pictures show? How do you know?

WELCOME TO Washington, D.C.

Maps help us find where we are.

In the city people ride trains to and from work.

Olmsted Walk
American Prairie
Cheetah
Conservation Station
Restrooms
Visitor Center

Signs help us find our way around the Zoo.

People enjoy nature in parks near the city.

The Washington Monument is one of the famous monuments in this city.

Farmers grow fruits and vegetables on their farms. Then they bring them to markets to sell.

Using Maps

Words to Know

map
Earth
globe

Look at the model of the playground below. A model is a copy of something.

Look at the **map** of the playground below. A map is a drawing of a place.

How are the map and model alike?

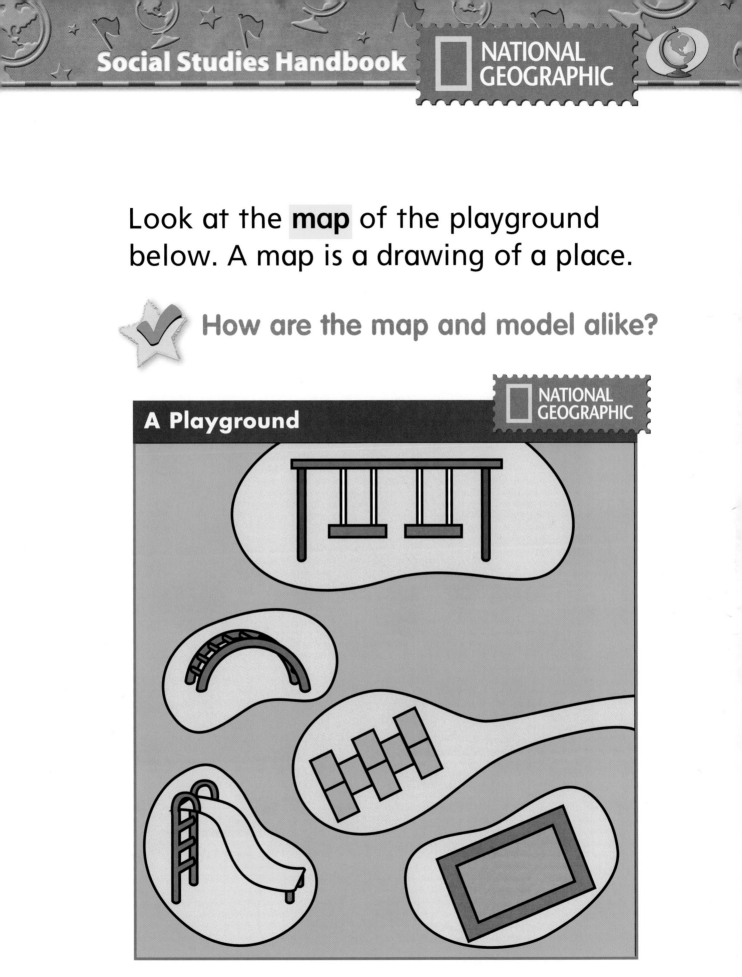

A Playground

NATIONAL GEOGRAPHIC

Using Globes

Earth is our home. It is round, like a ball. It is made up of land and water. This is a photo of Earth from space.

Earth

A **globe** is a model of Earth.
Globes show where land and
water are. They help you see
what Earth is like.

Globe

✓ **What do globes show?**

Literature

Hooray for Saturday!

by Becky Manfredini
and Jenny Reznick

illustrated by
Cathy Diefendorf

Many families like to stay together on Saturday.

Some families have picnics and play basketball.

Some families ride bikes with wheels big and small.

Some families do chores
and have lots of fun.

Some families help others
as they join in a run.

Whatever they do,
families will say,
"Let us spend time together.
Hooray for Saturday!"

Talk about it!

What does your family do on Saturdays?

All About Families

Take a LOOK

This family is having fun. How does your family have fun?

Explore more about families at our
Web site **www.mhschool.com**

What is a Family?

A **family** is a group of people who care for one another. Read about May's family.

"My family helps me learn and grow."

"I share special times
with my family."

"My family
cares for me."

There are many kinds
of families. In this unit
you will read more
about families.

Words to Know
About Families

Find the pictures
and say the words.

family

celebrate

holiday

transportation

Talk about it!

What do you see in this picture?

Many Families

My name is Chris. My family cares for one another. I show that I care by helping my family.

14

My mom and dad go to work. I go to school.

 How does Chris help his family?

Mary's Family

My name is Mary. My family has fun together.

My mom works at home. She takes care of my brother.

How does Mary have fun with her family?

Think and Write!

1. How are these families alike? How are they different?

2. How are these families like your family?

17

Families Celebrate

Families **celebrate** special times. To celebrate means to do something special.

A New Baby

A Graduation

Some families live far apart. They get together to celebrate.

Family Reunion

 What special times do families celebrate?

Special Days

A **holiday** is a special day. Read how these children celebrate holidays in December.

Kwanzaa

"We celebrate for seven days. We light a candle for every day."

20

Christmas

"We celebrate on December 25. We put lights on the tree."

Hanukkah

"We celebrate for eight days. We light a candle each night."

How does each family celebrate?

Think and Write!

1 What does it mean to celebrate?

2 How do you celebrate a holiday with your family?

Celebrate Families
with a Poem

Pride
by Alma Flor Ada

Proud of my family

Proud of my language

Proud of my culture

Proud of my people

Proud of being who I am.

22

Orgullo

Orgullosa de mi familia

Orgullosa de mi lengua

Orgullosa de mi cultura

Orgullosa de mi raza

Orgullosa de ser quien soy.

23

Where Families Live

Families live in many kinds of homes. Some families live in buildings with other families. Some families live in houses.

How are these homes alike?

Homes Around the World

Some families live in houses far away from one another. Some families live in houses close together.

Chile

Greece

Hong Kong, China

Morocco

How are these homes like
ones in your neighborhood?

Think and Write!

1. Where do families live?

2. How are the homes in this lesson
   different from each other?

Using Addresses

Grace is going to Stephen's house to play ball. Stephen lives in the white house. His **address** is 9 Elm Street.

An address tells you where someone lives. The first part is the building number. The second part is the street name.

The number 9 stands for the building number. Elm Street is the street name.

Try The Skill

1. What is the address of the yellow house?

2. What does the first part of an address tell you?

Make It!

Draw a picture of your school. Write its address below the picture.

Family Rules

Tim's family has **rules**. Rules tell us what we should do. Rules also tell us what we should not do. Tim's mother and father make the rules.

 What are rules?

Rules in the Home

One rule is that everyone helps at dinner.

Tim	sets table.
Dad	cooks dinner.
Mom	puts food away.
Sara	washes dishes.

Tim's family also has rules to keep him safe.

Tim and his sister have rules to help them get along. One rule is to play nicely together.

Name a rule in Tim's family.

Think and Write!

1. Who makes the rules in Tim's family?

2. What rules does your family have?

33

Problem Solving

A **problem** is something you need to think about. To **solve** a problem means to find an answer. There are three steps to solving a problem.

Step 1: Name the problem.
John forgot to bring a snack to school.

Step 2: List different choices.
John could ask his teacher to call his mom. John could wait until he gets home for a snack. John could ask a friend to share.

Step 3: Think and solve the problem. John wants to eat a snack now. It would take too long for his mom to bring a snack. He asks his friend Paul to share.

Try The Skill

1. What does it mean to solve a problem?

2. What is the first step in solving a problem?

3. Name a problem and tell how you solved it.

 Families on the Move

Jen and her family like to go to the park. Sometimes they take a bus.

Buses and trains are kinds of **transportation**. Transportation moves people or things from one place to another.

What kinds of transportation do you see in this picture?

PARK 333

1009

Transportation Then and Now

Bikes are another kind of transportation. Bikes have changed. They were bigger in the past. Now they are smaller.

Cars have changed, too. They used to be slow. Now they are faster.

How are cars today different from cars in the past?

Think and Write!

1 What is transportation?

2 What kinds of transportation does your family use?

Using Charts

Charts use words and pictures to show things. The title tells you what the chart is about. This chart is about how Mike gets to his favorite places.

Transportation to Mike's Favorite Places				
	bike	car	bus	airplane
park	X			
beach		X	X	
school	X	X	X	
grandparents				X

40

Read the top row of the chart. It names the kinds of transportation Mike uses.

Put your finger on the word "park." Now move your finger across the chart. The x on the chart means that Mike rides his bike to the park.

Try The Skill

1. What kinds of transportation does Mike use to get to school?

2. How does Mike visit his grandparents?

 Make a chart for the transportation you use.

6 Families and Change

Long ago, families washed clothes by hand. They used a washboard to get the dirt out. It took a long time.

Times have changed! Today most families use a washing machine. Families can wash more clothes in less time.

 How do most families wash their clothes today?

Sending Messages

Long ago, families did not have telephones. They wrote letters. It could take weeks to send a letter by mail.

Pony Express

Today, we can talk on the telephone or by computer.

Read the chart on the next page. It shows how sending messages has changed.

Ways to Send Messages

Long Ago	Today
Letter	Letter
	Telephone
	Computer

Chart Skill

How are messages sent today?

Think and Write!

1 How did families wash clothes long ago?

2 How has the way families stay in touch changed?

45

Biography

Thomas Edison

Thomas Edison made many new things. One was the light bulb.

phonograph

Read what Thomas Edison said about his light bulb.

In his own words

> **"Everyone will wonder why they never thought of it, it is so simple."**
> —Thomas Edison

Families today still use things Edison made.

light bulb

 Explore the life of Thomas Edison at our Web site www.mhschool.com

Being a Good Citizen

Helping Kids Have Fun

Spencer Whale lives in Pittsburgh, Pennsylvania. He saw children in a hospital. They needed something to carry their medicine when they played.

Spencer made a toy car that carries the medicine. Now the children can play on their own.

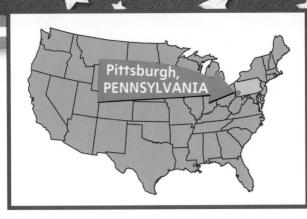

Pittsburgh, PENNSYLVANIA

Spencer says, "I was happy because the kids have more fun."

Spencer Whale

Why is it important to help others?

Activity

What could you make to help others? Draw a picture of it.

A Look at a Family
Celebrating in Kenya

Jomo lives in a country named Kenya. Today is a special day. He will celebrate Jamuhuri Day. On this day, people in Kenya celebrate freedom.

Nairobi

Jomo's family will watch a parade in the city of Nairobi. They will hear music. At home Jomo's family will have a special meal.

Talk about it!

How does Jomo's family celebrate Jamuhuri Day?

Words to Know

Match the words to the pictures.

holiday   transportation   family

1.

2.

3.

Check Your Reading

4. What is a holiday that you celebrate?

5. Why do families have rules?

6. How are families alike? How are they different?

Using Charts

Look at the chart below.

7. Who takes out the trash?

8. Who sets the table for dinner?

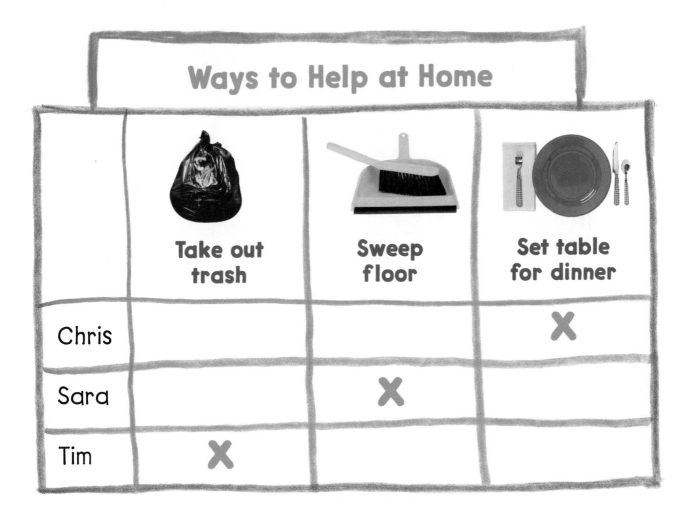

Ways to Help at Home

	Take out trash	Sweep floor	Set table for dinner
Chris			X
Sara		X	
Tim	X		

 Make a chart that shows how you help at home.

Using Addresses

Look at the picture. Kim lives in this house.

9. What is Kim's address?

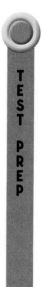

Problem Solving

10. Which picture shows the problem?

Activity

Make a Rules Mobile

* Draw three pictures of rules that you follow at home.

* Hang up your pictures.

Think and Write!

How do people in your family show that they care about each other?

To learn more about this unit, visit our Web site at **www.mhschool.com**

Literature

The Legend of Johnny Appleseed

by Nathan Jaffe
illustrated by Linda Hill Griffith

Once there was a man named John Chapman. John had many apple seeds. He looked for places to plant the seeds. He walked all over the land.

John found some land to plant his seeds. His seeds grew into beautiful apple trees.

John gave seeds to people he met. Soon there were apple trees everywhere.

The people thanked John. They called him Johnny Appleseed.

Talk about it!

How did Johnny Appleseed change our land?

Where We Live

Take a LOOK

This family is at a park. What special places are near your home?

Explore geography at our Web site
www.mhschool.com

What is Geography?

Geography tells you where places are and what they are like. See how Will learns about geography.

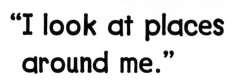

San Francisco

"I look at places around me."

"I look at maps and globes."

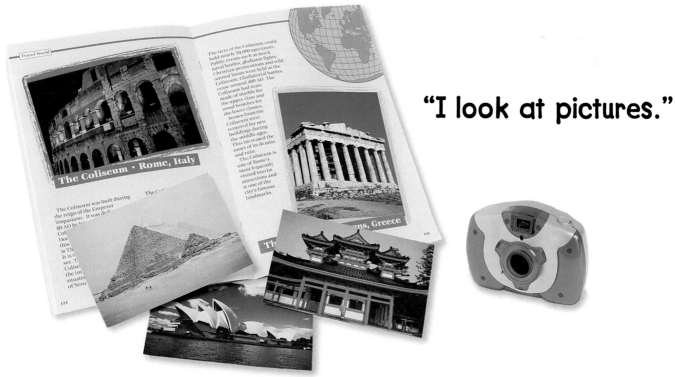

"I look at pictures."

In this unit you will read more about geography.

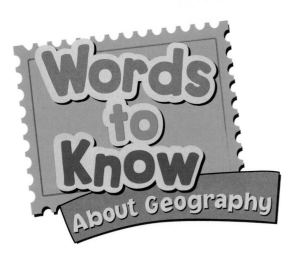
Words to Know
About Geography

Find the pictures
and say the words.

mountain

city

river

farm

weather

Talk about it!

What do you see in this picture?

Lesson 1

We Live in Communities

We all live in **communities**. A community is a place where people live, work, and play.

Words to Know

community
city
neighbor
farm

A **city** is a big community. These children live in the city of Chicago, Illinois.

 What is a community?

Town Life

A town is a small community. Joe and Bill live in the town of Clovis, California.

They live near each other. They are **neighbors**.

Bill's house

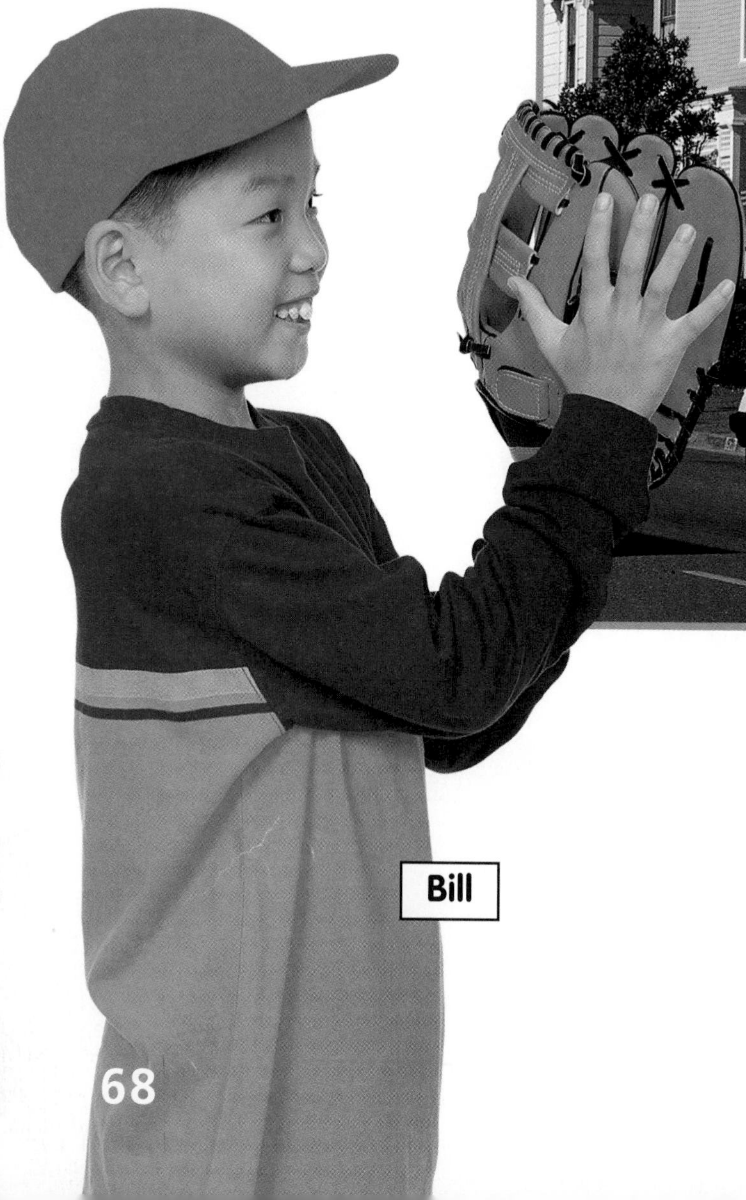

Bill

Joe's house

Clovis, CALIFORNIA

Joe

What is a neighbor?

69

Life on a Farm

Meet Sara. She lives on a **farm** near Lewisburg, West Virginia. A farm is a place where people raise animals and grow plants.

Sara

The farms in Sara's community are far apart. Sara's neighbor is Maria.

What is a farm?

Maria

Think and Write!

1. How are the communities in this lesson alike? How are they different?

2. What is your community like?

71

Using Pictures and Maps

Ajay's community looks like this from an airplane.

A map is a drawing of a place. Look at the map of Ajay's community on the next page.

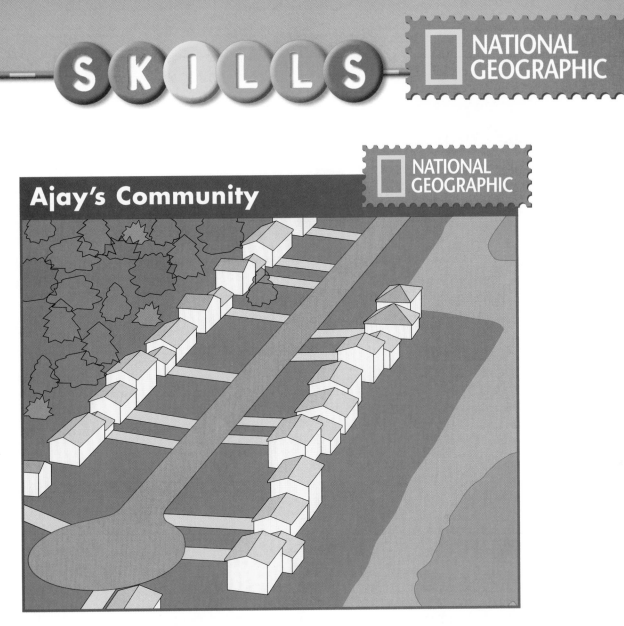

Ajay's Community

NATIONAL GEOGRAPHIC

Point to the water in the photo.
Now find it on the map.

Try The Skill

1. Look at the map. Is the water to the right or left of the houses?

2. How is the map like the picture? How is it different?

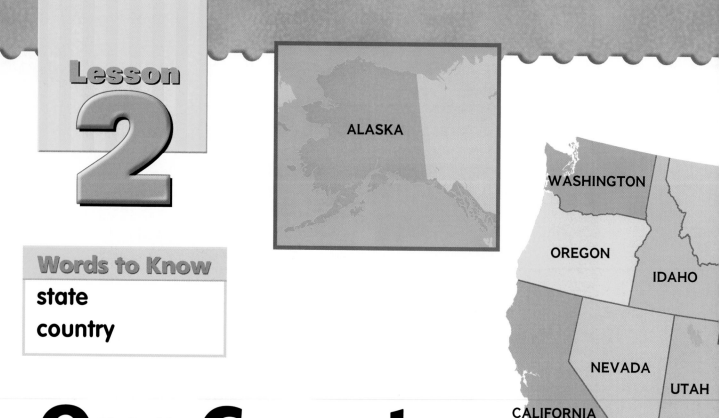

Words to Know

state

country

Our Country

Communities are in a bigger place called a **state**. This map shows 50 states. States make up our **country**. A country is a land and the people who live there. Our country is the United States of America.
Find your state on the map.

74

The United States of America

NATIONAL GEOGRAPHIC

MAINE
VERMONT
NEW HAMPSHIRE
MASSACHUSETTS
RHODE ISLAND
CONNECTICUT
NEW JERSEY
DELAWARE

MONTANA
NORTH DAKOTA
MINNESOTA
SOUTH DAKOTA
WISCONSIN
MICHIGAN
NEW YORK
PENNSYLVANIA
WYOMING
IOWA
NEBRASKA
OHIO
MARYLAND
INDIANA
ILLINOIS
WEST VIRGINIA
VIRGINIA
COLORADO
KANSAS
MISSOURI
KENTUCKY
NORTH CAROLINA
OKLAHOMA
TENNESSEE
SOUTH CAROLINA
NEW MEXICO
ARKANSAS
MISSISSIPPI
GEORGIA
ALABAMA
TEXAS
LOUISIANA
FLORIDA

⦿ Map Skill

What state is above Arkansas?

Think and Write! ✎

1 **What is the full name of our country?**

2 **What other states touch your state?**

75

Sorting into Groups

Tim and his family took a trip across our country. Look at the pictures of his trip on the next page.

Tim **sorted** his pictures. To sort means to put things that are alike into a group.

Tim put the three pictures of cities into one group.

Try The Skill

1. What groups could you make from the other six pictures?

2. How are the pictures in each group alike?

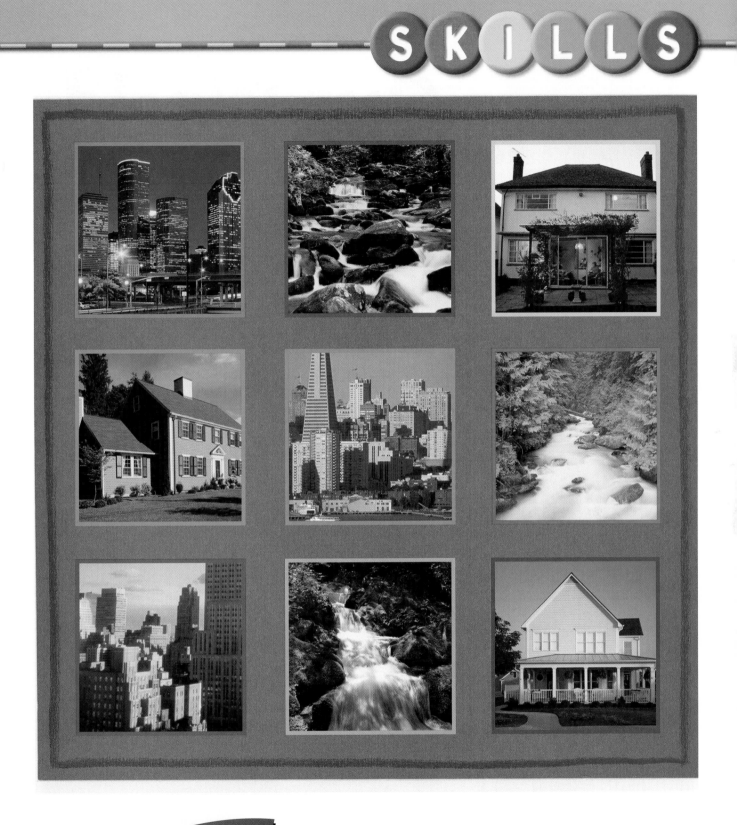

 What can you sort in your classroom?

Our World

Our country is part of a **continent**. A continent is a very large body of land. Our country is part of a continent called North America.

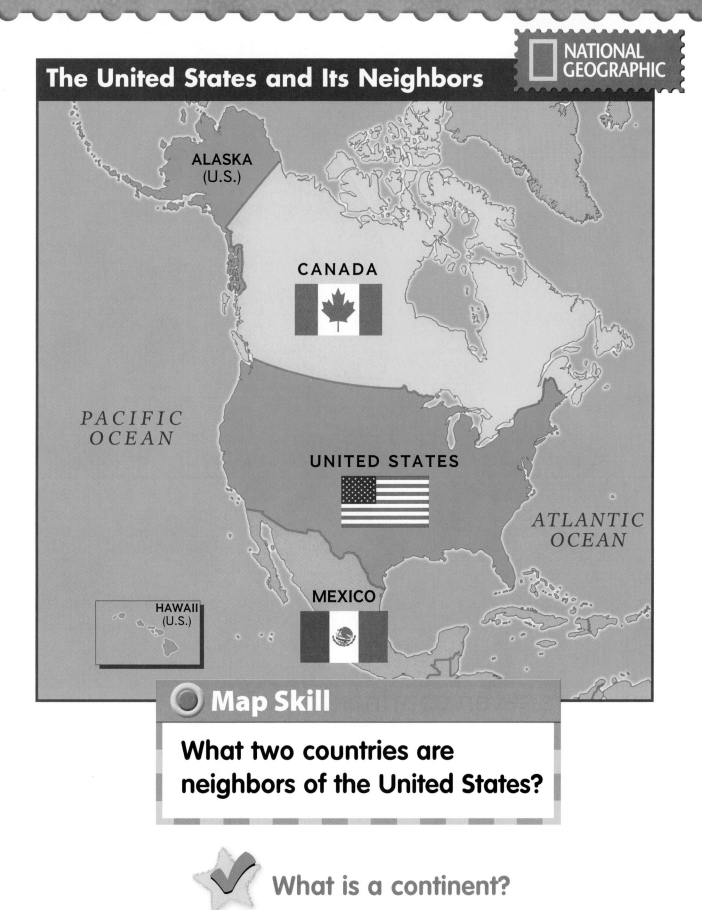

The United States and Its Neighbors

NATIONAL GEOGRAPHIC

ALASKA
(U.S.)

CANADA

PACIFIC
OCEAN

UNITED STATES

ATLANTIC
OCEAN

HAWAII
(U.S.)

MEXICO

◉ Map Skill

What two countries are neighbors of the United States?

✓ What is a continent?

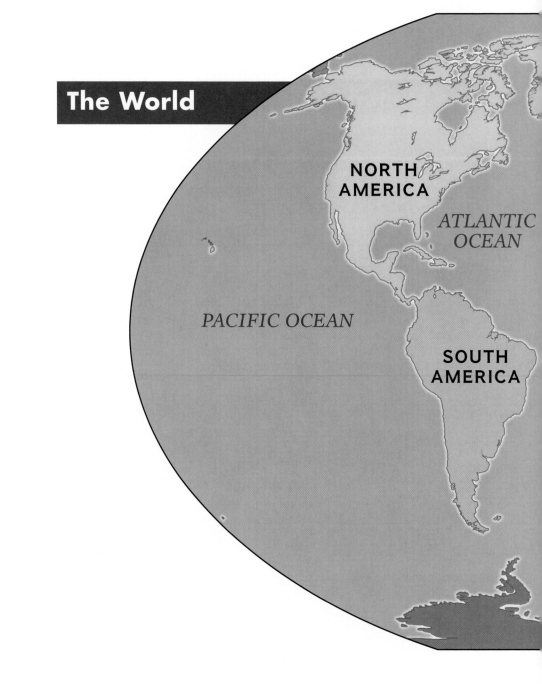

The World

NORTH
AMERICA

ATLANTIC
OCEAN

PACIFIC OCEAN

SOUTH
AMERICA

Earth

There are seven continents on Earth.
Earth is our world. Earth is made up
of land and water. **Oceans** are large
bodies of water around the continents.

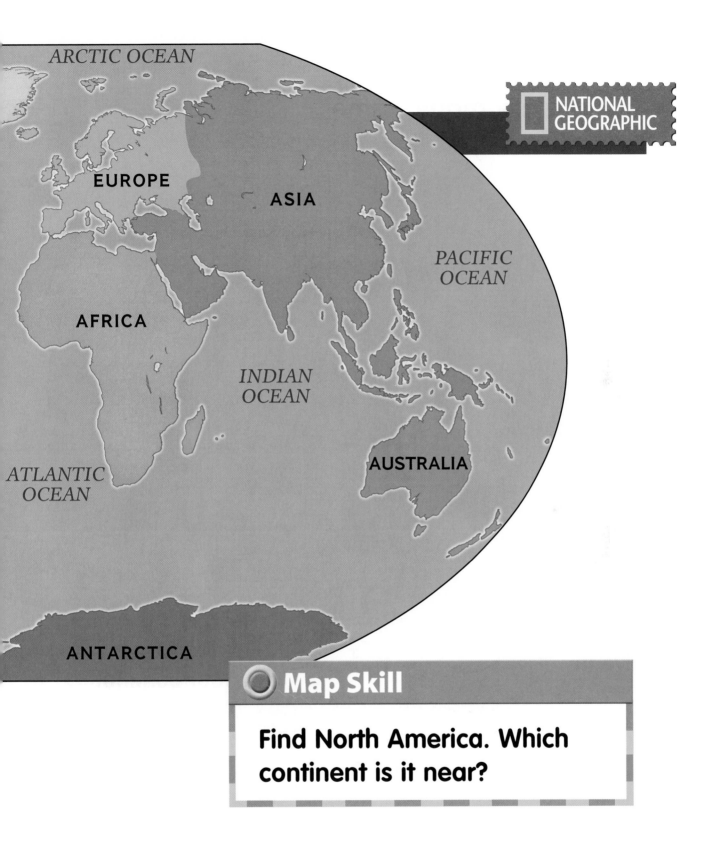

ARCTIC OCEAN

NATIONAL GEOGRAPHIC

EUROPE

ASIA

PACIFIC OCEAN

AFRICA

INDIAN OCEAN

ATLANTIC OCEAN

AUSTRALIA

ANTARCTICA

○ **Map Skill**

Find North America. Which continent is it near?

 Name three continents on Earth.

Where You Live

There are many names
for where you live.

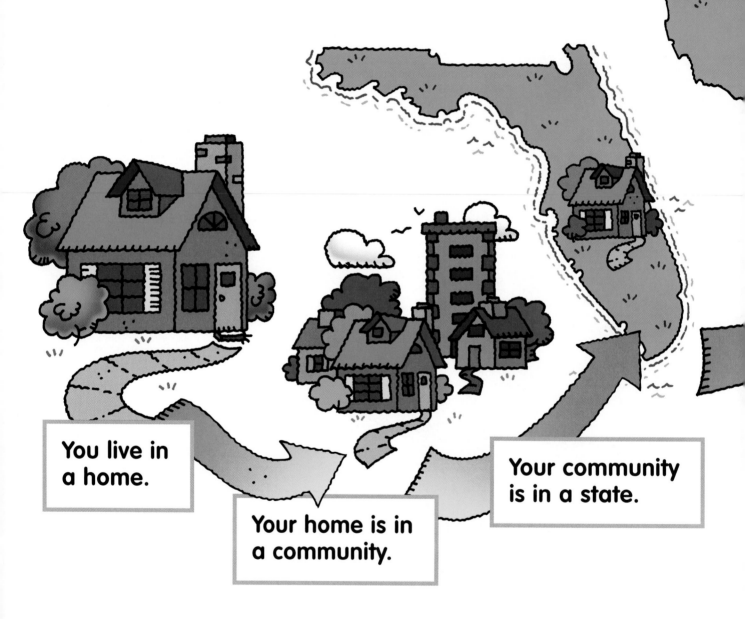

You live in
a home.

Your home is in
a community.

Your community
is in a state.

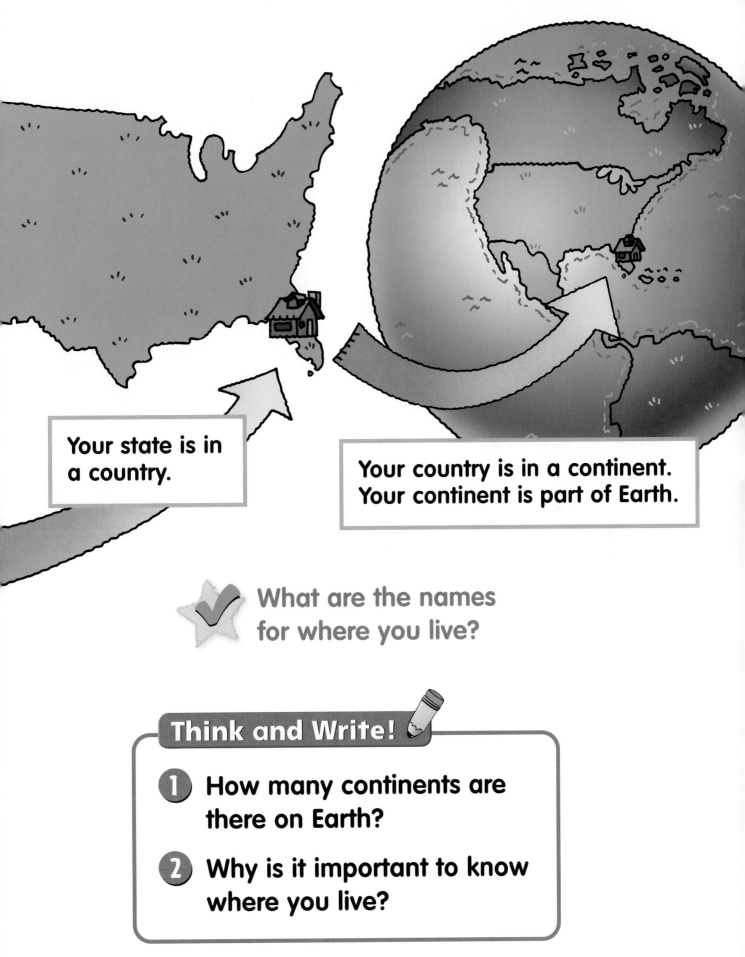

Your state is in a country.

Your country is in a continent.
Your continent is part of Earth.

What are the names for where you live?

Think and Write!

1. How many continents are there on Earth?

2. Why is it important to know where you live?

Celebrate Our World with a Song

Big Beautiful Planet

Words and Music by Raffi

Refrain

F   Gm   F

There's a big beauti-ful plan-et in the sky, _____

Gm   F

And it's my home, _____ It's where I live.

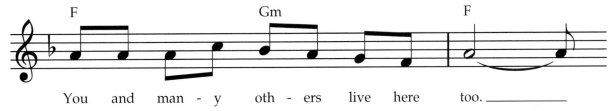

You and man - y oth - ers live here too. _____

The earth is our home, _____ It's where we live. _____

Water and Land

Words to Know
lake
river
plain
hill
mountain

Earth is made of water and land.

Oceans are the largest bodies of water. The Pacific Ocean is the largest ocean on Earth.

A **lake** is a body of water with land all around it. There are many lakes in the state of Minnesota.

A **river** flows across the land. The Mississippi River is the largest river in our country.

 Name two bodies of water.

Different Kinds of Land

Flat land is called a **plain**. The state of Iowa is part of a big plain. This plain is the biggest in our country.

A **hill** is land higher than the land around it. There are many hills in the state of Idaho.

Mountains are the highest kind of land. Mt. McKinley is the tallest mountain in North America.

Name two kinds of land.

Mt. McKinley

Think and Write!

1 What is a plain?

2 How are lakes and rivers different?

Using Map Keys

Symbols are drawings that stand for real things. This blue circle stands for a lake.

A **map key** tells you what the symbols on a map mean.

Point to the lake symbol in the map key. Find the lake symbol on the map. It tells you that there is a lake near the farm.

A Country Community

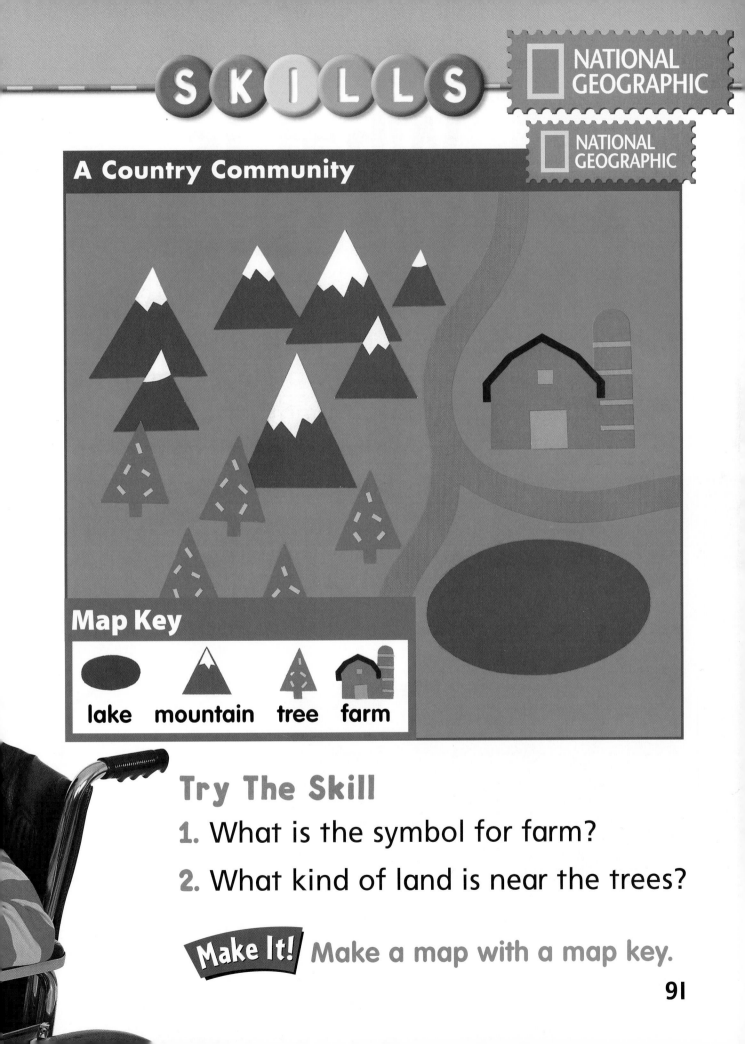

Map Key

lake   mountain   tree   farm

Try The Skill

1. What is the symbol for farm?

2. What kind of land is near the trees?

Make It! Make a map with a map key.

91

What is Weather?

Words to Know

weather

season

Weather is what it is like outside. Two places can have different weather at the same time. One place is cold. Another place might be hot.

Amy lives in Texas. Her friend Roberta lives in Washington.

◉ Using Charts

Look at the chart. It shows the weather in the states of Washington and Texas over three days.

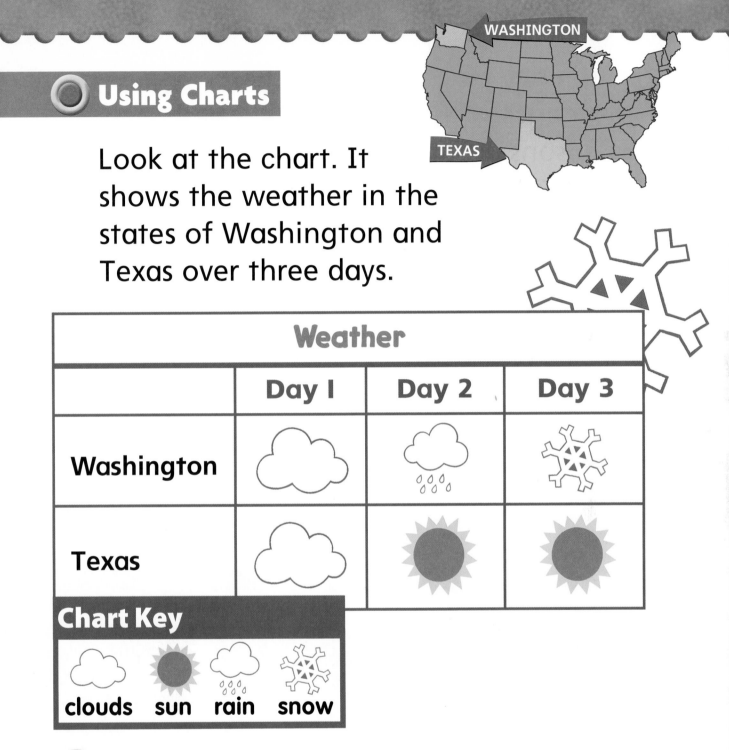

Weather			
	Day 1	**Day 2**	**Day 3**
Washington	clouds	rain	snow
Texas	clouds	sun	sun

Chart Key

clouds   sun   rain   snow

◉ Chart Skill

What was the weather in Texas when it snowed in Washington?

✔ What is weather?

Four Seasons

In many places, the weather changes with the **seasons**. The seasons are spring, summer, fall, and winter.

We can do different things each season.

Spring

Summer

Fall

Winter

What things do you
do each season?

Think and Write!

1. Name the four seasons.

2. Why is it important to know
what the weather is?

Caring for Our Natural Resources

We all need air and water to stay alive. Air and water are **natural resources**. Natural resources are things in nature that people use.

Plants are another natural resource. The food from plants helps us grow. Plants also keep the air clean.

 Name two natural resources.

States Have Natural Resources

Coal and oil are natural resources. They come from under the ground. Coal and oil warm our homes and schools. Oil is used to make gas. Gas makes our cars run.

Every state has special natural resources. Look at the map of the state of Kentucky. What resources does Kentucky have? trees, oil, gas and coal

coal

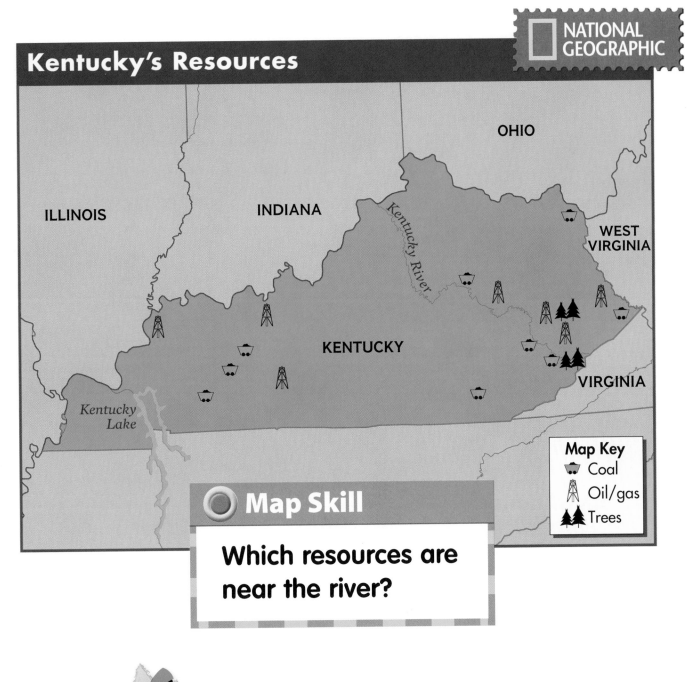

NATIONAL GEOGRAPHIC

Kentucky's Resources

OHIO

ILLINOIS

INDIANA

Kentucky River

WEST VIRGINIA

KENTUCKY

VIRGINIA

Kentucky Lake

Map Key
Coal
Oil/gas
Trees

⬤ **Map Skill**

Which resources are near the river?

✔ How do we use coal and oil?

99

Taking Care of Our World

Everyone needs to take care of our natural resources. Our natural resources will not last without our care.

There are many things we can do to help. We can use things over and over. We can keep our land and water clean. We can make art out of old things.

 What can we do to take care of our natural resources?

Think and Write!

1 **What are natural resources?**

2 **Why must we take care of our natural resources?**

Biography

Rachel Carson

Rachel Carson liked to read books. She also loved nature. She wrote a book about nature.

SILENT SPRING

WITH AN INTRODUCTION BY VICE PRESIDENT Al Gore

RACHEL CARSON

Rachel Carson worked hard to help Earth. She helped to take care of our natural resources.

Read what she said about her work.

In her own words

"Now I can believe I have at least helped a little."

—Rachel Carson

Explore the life of Rachel Carson at our Web site www.mhschool.com

Making Decisions

Keeping our World Clean

Rachel Carson cared about our world. We care about our world, too. Look at these pictures. What decision would you make?

I do not want this.

APPLE JUICE

104

I did not make this mess.

How could these children be good citizens? Ask a parent, teacher, or other adult.

Activity

Clean up a part of your school. Take before and after photos. Hang them on the classroom wall.

A Look at Geography in Switzerland

Switzerland is a country in Europe. It has many beautiful mountains and lakes. Many of the mountains are covered with snow.

Some Swiss people live in the mountains. Some live in towns.

Talk about it!

What makes up the geography of Switzerland?

Words to Know

Use these words to finish the sentences.

weather city geography

1. A ____ is a community where many people live, work, and play.

2. I look at maps and globes to learn about ____ .

3. ____ is what it is like outside.

Check Your Reading

4. How are cities and farms different? How are they alike?

5. How are the seasons different? How are they alike?

6. Why are natural resources important to people?

Using Maps and Map Keys

7. Are the houses left or right of the river?

8. What is the symbol for school?

9. What body of water is next to the houses?

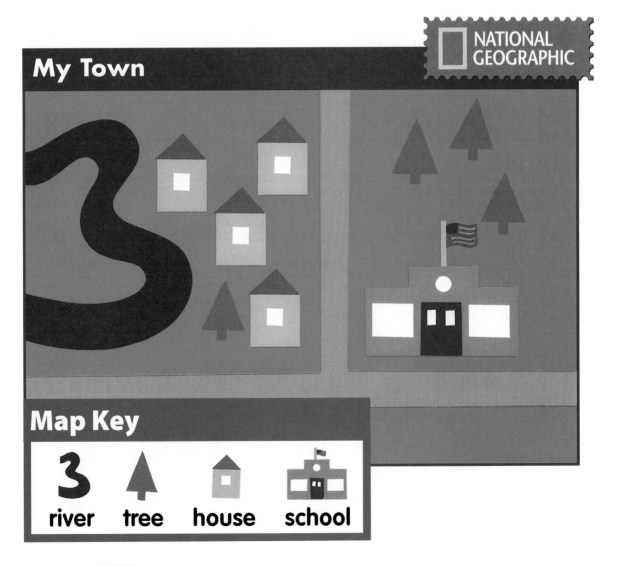

Make It! Make a map of your community.

Sorting into Groups

Look at the pictures below.
Then answer the question.

10. Which picture does not belong in the group?

Activity

Make a "My Earth" Banner

* Make a picture of how you take care of Earth.

* Write about what you do below your picture.

Think and Write

Why is it important to know about your world?

To learn more about this unit, visit our Web site at **www.mhschool.com**

Literature

A Good Helper

by Madeline Willis

illustrated by
Karen Brooks

I am a good helper
in all that I do.
I help my neighbors
and community, too.

113

I make sure to throw my trash away.
I put my cans in the bin every day.

When I am in class or
in the hall,
I open the doors for
one and all!

When I am at school,
   I remember to share.
I follow class rules
   to show that I care.

I help other people.
   I help those in need.
I feel proud of myself
   when I do a good deed!

Talk about it!

How do you help other people?

Good Citizens

Take a LOOK

These children are saying the Pledge of Allegiance. They care about our country. How do you show you care?

Explore good citizenship at our
Web site **www.mhschool.com**

The Big Idea

What Makes a Good Citizen?

A **citizen** is a person who belongs to a country. Being a good citizen is important. Read how Sue is a good citizen.

"I get along with my classmates."

"I follow rules."

"I help other people."

In this unit you will read about being good citizens.

Find the pictures
and say the words.

flag

President

group

vote

Talk about it!

What do you see in this picture?

People Get Along

Words to Know

group

People who do things together make up a **group**.

Did you know you belonged to many groups? Your class is a group. Your family is also a group.

124

People in groups work together. To get along, they listen to each other. They share. They make plans together.

Name two groups you belong to.

Classroom Rules

Rules help people to get along.
Your teacher makes rules for
your classroom.

Read the chart about rules
on the next page.

Classroom Rules

Raise your hand in class.	Put away your things.	Walk. Do not run.
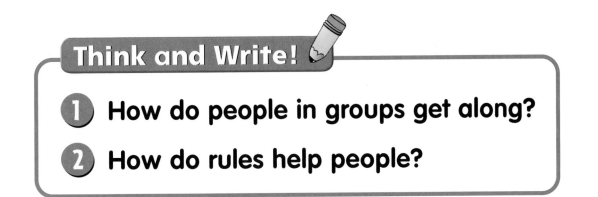		

 Chart Skill

Name two rules for getting along.

Think and Write!

1 How do people in groups get along?

2 How do rules help people?

Using Directions

North, south, east, and west are four **directions** on Earth. They help you find places on maps.

When you face north, west is to your left. What direction is to your right?

North Pole

North

West

East

South

Try The Skill

1. Look at the map on the next page. Is the globe east or west of the reading rug?

2. Point to the class pet. Is it north or south of the teacher's desk?

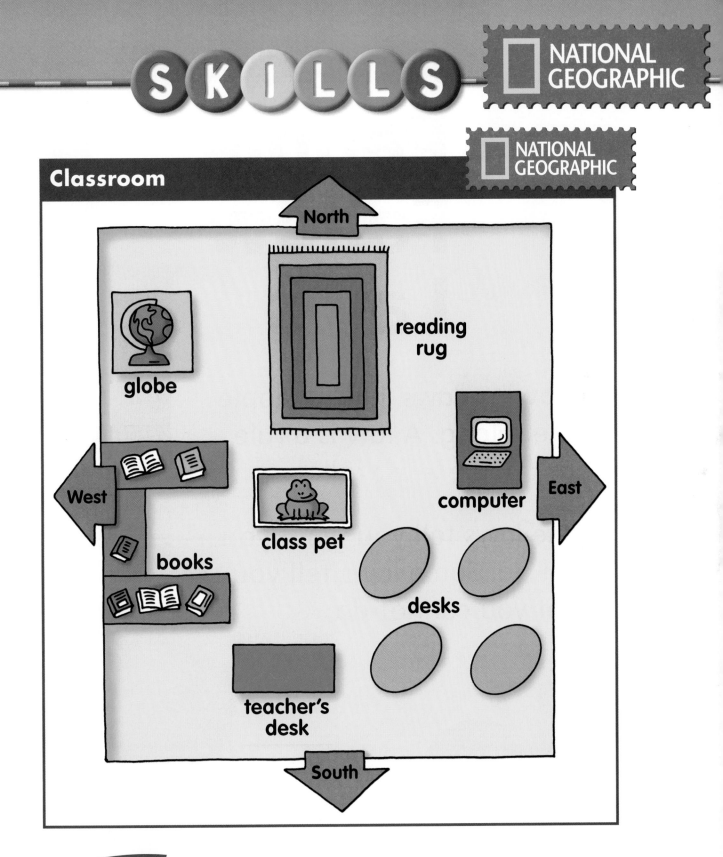

Classroom

- North
- South
- East
- West
- globe
- reading rug
- computer
- class pet
- books
- desks
- teacher's desk

 **Make It!** Make a map of your classroom. Add arrows to show the four directions.

2

People Follow Laws

Following **laws** helps people to get along. A law is a rule that people must follow.

Some laws tell you what you must do. Some laws tell you what you cannot do.

Cars must stop when they see a stop light. This law makes it safe to cross the street.

Think and Write!

1. How do laws help us?

2. Name a law that keeps you safe.

Lesson 3

What is a Leader?

Words to Know

leader
mayor
governor
President

A **leader** is someone who helps us to make plans. A good leader helps us to do the right thing.

Your teacher is a leader in your classroom. Your teacher helps you to learn.

Police officers are also leaders. They help to make your community safe.

 What is a good leader?

Leaders in Our Country

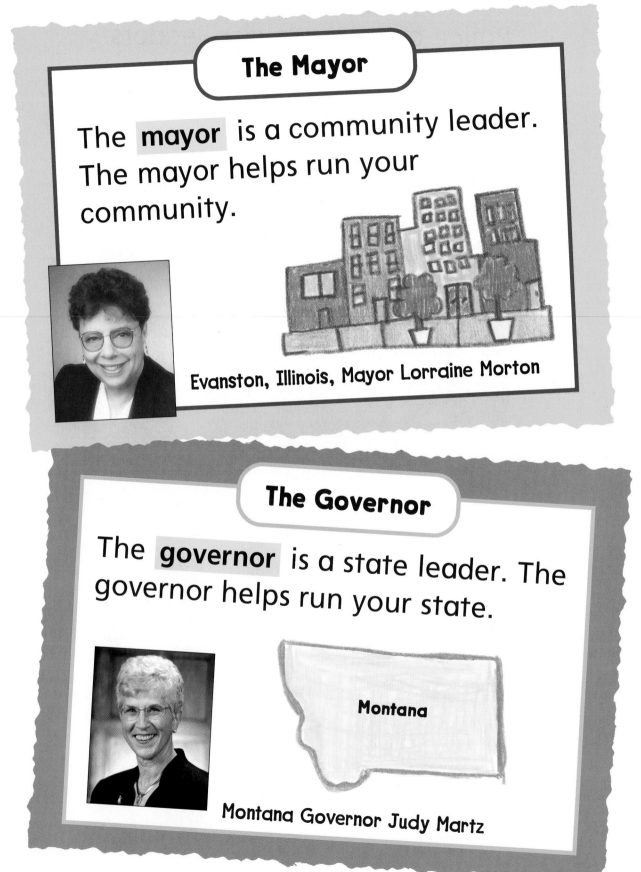

The Mayor

The **mayor** is a community leader. The mayor helps run your community.

Evanston, Illinois, Mayor Lorraine Morton

The Governor

The **governor** is a state leader. The governor helps run your state.

Montana

Montana Governor Judy Martz

The President

The **President** is the leader of our country. The President helps run our country. The President lives in Washington,D.C.

United States
President
George W. Bush

Washington, D.C.

✓ What does a mayor do?

Think and Write!

1 Name two leaders.

2 Why are good leaders important?

Biography

Mary McLeod Bethune

Mary McLeod Bethune started schools for African Americans. She wanted all people to be able to go to school.

Mary Bethune was a leader. She was friends with Eleanor Roosevelt. They worked together. Mary Bethune made America a better place.

Mary McLeod Bethune with Eleanor Roosevelt

Explore more about the life of Mary McLeod Bethune at our Web site www.mhschool.com

Being a Good Citizen

Getting Along at School

Ms. Cater's class is in Oakland, California. In her class, everyone learns rules for getting along. One rule is no put-downs. Carlos Reyes says, "This means not calling people names."

Oakland, CALIFORNIA

Another rule is to talk it out. Dalia Jasso says, "We try to talk instead of fight."

Dalia and Carlos want everyone in their class to get along.

Carlos Alfredo Reyes

Dalia Jasso Silva

⭐ Be a Good Citizen

What rules help you get along with other people in your school?

Activity

Make a bulletin board of your classroom rules.

139

Votes Count!

Sometimes we want to do different things. How do we decide what to do? We **vote**. To vote means to choose something. Voting is a fair way to make plans.

Steve and his friends want to play together. Some of them want to play soccer. Some of them want to play ball. They take a vote.

Think and Write!

1. Why do we sometimes need to vote?

2. Name a choice your class could make by taking a vote.

Our Symbols and Pledge

Words to Know

flag

Many different people live in the United States. Together we make one country. We have a saying for this. It is *E pluribus unum*. That means, "Out of Many, One."

E pluribus unum

Our **flag** is a symbol for our country. A symbol stands for something else. Our flag is red, white, and blue. It has 50 stars. Each of the stars stands for one of the 50 states.

 What does our flag stand for?

Our Song and the Pledge

We are proud of our flag.
We have a song for it called
The Star-Spangled Banner.
We also say the *Pledge of
Allegiance*. It is a promise
to be a good citizen.

Read the Pledge of Allegiance.

I pledge allegiance to the flag of the United States of America and to the Republic for which it stands, one Nation under God, indivisible, with liberty and justice for all.

 Why do we say the Pledge of Allegiance?

Bald Eagle

The bald eagle is a symbol. It stands for our country. It makes us feel proud to be Americans.

The Liberty Bell

The Liberty Bell is another symbol. It rang long ago when the United States became a country. The Liberty Bell is in Philadelphia, Pennsylvania.

 What do the bald eagle and Liberty Bell stand for?

The Statue of Liberty

The Statue of Liberty is a symbol. It stands for hope. It has welcomed new people to our country for a long time. The statue is in New York Harbor.

Uncle Sam

Uncle Sam is another symbol for our country. He wears red, white, and blue. Uncle Sam helps us celebrate America!

 Why are the Statue of Liberty and Uncle Sam special?

Think and Write!

1 **Name three American symbols.**

2 **Why are you proud to be an American?**

Using the Calendar

Calendars are charts that show the months of a year. They show the weeks in a month. They also show the days in a week. Calendars show holidays, too.

Look at the title of the calendar. It shows the month of July. Point to the square with the number four. It stands for one day. This is July 4th.

Try The Skill

1. How many days are in July?

2. What day of the week is July 4th?

 Make a calendar showing what you did yesterday. Show what you will do today and tomorrow.

July

Sunday	Monday	Tuesday	Wednesday	Thursday	Friday	Saturday
		1	2	3	4 Independence Day	5
6	7	8	9	10	11	12
13 State Fair	14	15	16	17	18	19
20	21	22	23	24	25	26 Clean the Park Day
27	28	29	30 Dad's Birthday	31		

Good Citizens

Good citizens make our country a better place. They work to help others. You will read about good citizens in this lesson.

Nathan Hale was in the army. He worked to make America free. He gave his life for his country. Read what he said.

In his own words

"I only regret that I have but one life to lose for my country."

— Nathan Hale

Why is Nathan Hale special?

General George Washington and Nathan Hale

Frederick Douglass

Frederick Douglass lived many years ago. He was a slave, but ran away. He became a leader. He worked to free African Americans.

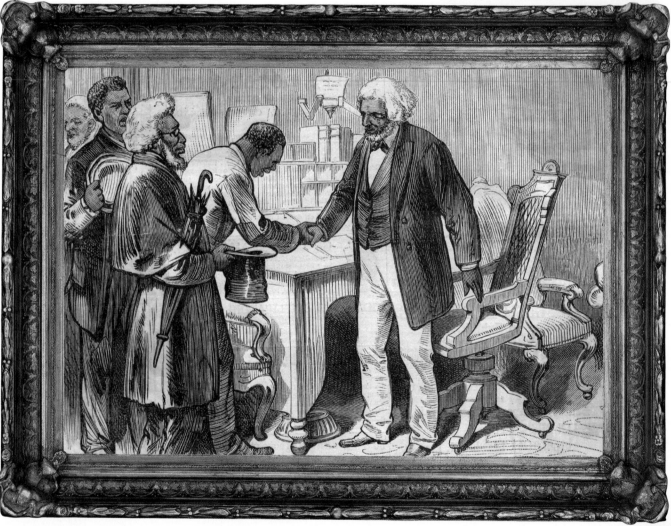

Clara Barton

Clara Barton helped soldiers who were hurt. She began the Red Cross in America. The Red Cross still helps people who are in need.

How were Clara Barton and Frederick Douglass good citizens?

Eleanor Roosevelt

Eleanor Roosevelt helped poor people. She worked so that life would be fair for everyone. Her husband was President Franklin D. Roosevelt.

Good citizens are around us everyday. You, too, can be a good citizen.

How was Eleanor Roosevelt a good citizen?

Think and Write!

1. How are the citizens in this lesson alike? How are they different?

2. How can you be a good citizen?

Celebrate America
With a Song

My Country, 'Tis of Thee

Music by Henry Carey
Words by Samuel F. Smith

My coun - try 'tis of thee, Sweet land of

lib - er - ty, Of thee I sing. Land where my

fa - thers died, Land of the Pil - grim's pride,

From ev' - ry ___ moun - tain-side Let ___ free - dom ring.

159

A Look at First Graders in Japan

In Japan, children bow to their teacher at the beginning of class. One child says, "Rei." This means bow. Then the children say, "Please teach us."

Children in Japan wear uniforms in school. In the afternoon they play. When school is over, the children walk home.

Talk about it!

How are children in Japan like children in America? How are they different?

Words to Know

Choose the word that best tells about each clue.

group citizen President

1. the leader of our country

2. people who do things together

3. a person who belongs to a country

Check Your Reading

4. How do groups get along?

5. Why is voting a good way to choose something?

6. Who is Uncle Sam?

Using Directions

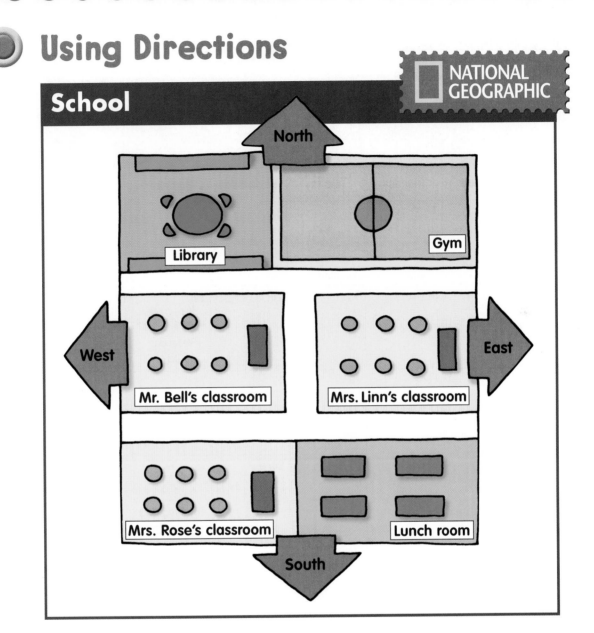

School

North

Library

Gym

West

Mr. Bell's classroom

Mrs. Linn's classroom

East

Mrs. Rose's classroom

Lunch room

South

7. Find the lunch room. Is it north or south of the gym?

8. What room is west of Mrs. Linn's classroom?

 Make a map of your school. Add arrows to show the four directions.

Using the Calendar

November

Sunday	Monday	Tuesday	Wednesday	Thursday	Friday	Saturday
	1	2 Election Day	3	4	5	6
7	8	9	10	11 Veterans Day	12	13
14	15	16	17	18	19	20
21 Amy's Birthday	22	23	24	25 Thanksgiving Day	26	27
28	29	30				

9. Thanksgiving Day is on a ____.

Friday   Wednesday   Thursday

10. Amy's birthday is on November ____.

20   21   28

Unit Activity

Make a Good Citizen Badge

* Make a badge using construction paper, scissors, and glue.

* Write "Good Citizen" on the round piece of paper.

* Write one way you are a good citizen on the ribbon.

 Think and Write

What makes a good citizen?

To learn more about this unit, visit our Web site at **www.mhschool.com**

Literature

The Ant and the Grasshopper

An Aesop's Fable

retold by Noah Michaels

illustrated by Linda Bild

One day, Grasshopper was having lots of fun. He was hopping and singing. He saw Ant.

Grasshopper said, "Come and have fun with me."

Ant said, "I am sorry, but I cannot. I have to put away food for winter. You should do the same."

Grasshopper said, "Why should I? I have enough food to eat for now."

So Grasshopper kept hopping and singing.

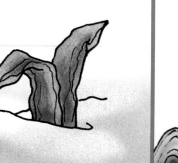

Winter came. There was no food for Grasshopper. He got hungry.

Grasshopper saw Ant sharing corn with the other ants. It was the corn Ant had put away in the summer! Then Grasshopper knew:

It is best to work hard and be prepared.

Talk about it!

What did Grasshopper learn from Ant?

4

All Kinds of Jobs

Take a LOOK

There are many kinds of jobs. What kinds of work do you know about?

Explore work at our Web site
www.mhschool.com

171

What is Work?

Work is a job that someone does. Read about the work that Lisa does.

"I do work to help my father."

172

"I do work at school."

"I do work with my sister."

In this unit you will read more about work and jobs.

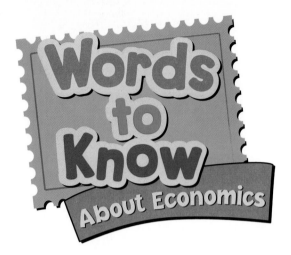
Words to Know

About Economics

Find the pictures and say the words.

services

goods

shelter

work

Pet Fair

Talk about it!

What do you see in this picture?

Needs and Wants

What are **needs**? Needs are things we must have to live. People need food and water.

176

People need **shelter**, too.
A shelter is a place to live.

People need clothes.
People also need love and
care. Families can help
meet these needs.

 What do people need?

Making Choices

Wants are things we would like to have. We cannot have all of our wants. We have to choose.

Sue and her family want to buy a computer. They also want new bikes. They cannot buy both.

Sue and her family have to decide what to buy. They already have bikes. They do not have a computer.

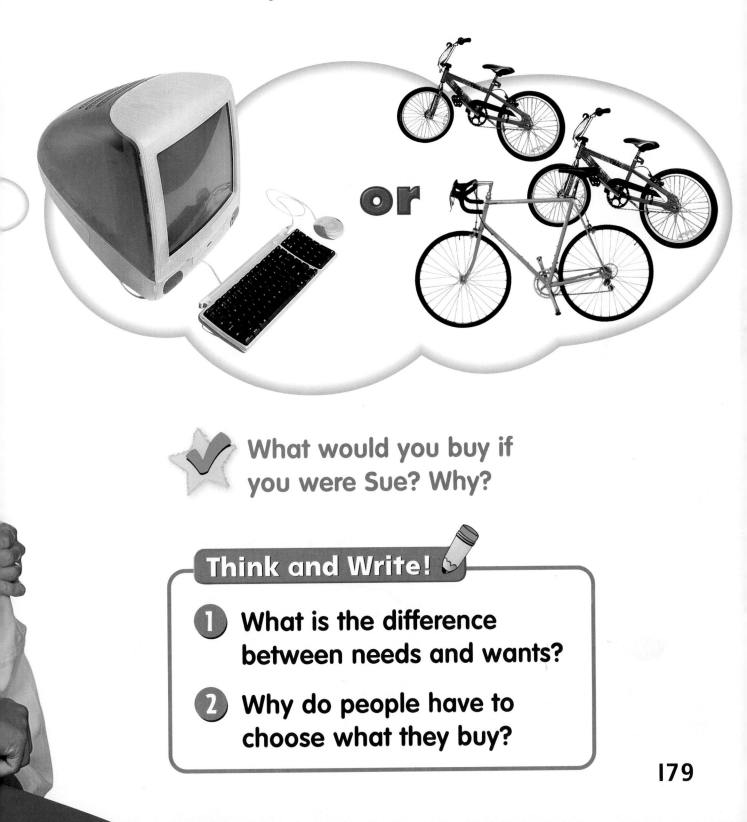

✓ **What would you buy if you were Sue? Why?**

Think and Write! ✏️

1 **What is the difference between needs and wants?**

2 **Why do people have to choose what they buy?**

o Know

er

Work and Jobs

It is important to do a good job. John works as a chef in a restaurant. He knows how to do many things at one time. John does his best to make good food.

How does John do a good job?

Many Jobs

There are many jobs. You could be a scientist or work in a shop.

People need to be able to read and write to do their jobs. Many people go to school to learn how to do their jobs.

Most people make money for doing their jobs. People use money to buy things.

Some people work without making money. They are called **volunteers**. Some volunteers help children learn how to read.

 How do some people learn how to do a job?

Think and Write!

1. Name three different types of jobs.

2. Why is it important to do your best at work?

Celebrate Work
with Art

These pictures were painted by William Gropper. They celebrate people working in America. What kinds of work are they doing?

"Automobile Industry" by William Gropper

**"Construction of the Dam"
by William Gropper**

Goods and Services

Goods are things that people make or grow. Food grown on a farm is one kind of good. Some food people eat comes from a farm.

Goods are also made in a building called a **factory**. Orange juice is made in a factory.

How are factories and farms alike?

Jobs That Help Others

Some people do things for other people. This work is called a **service**.

There are many service jobs. The cook brings you food. The dentist takes care of you.

Name a job that is a service.

Think and Write!

1. Name two kinds of goods.

2. Why are service jobs important?

Using Picture Graphs

A **picture graph** uses pictures to show numbers of things. The title tells you what the graph shows. Look at the picture graph on the next page. It shows how long it takes to paint different rooms.

Each paintbrush stands for one day. Count the paintbrushes next to the word "kitchen." There are three. It takes three days to paint the kitchen.

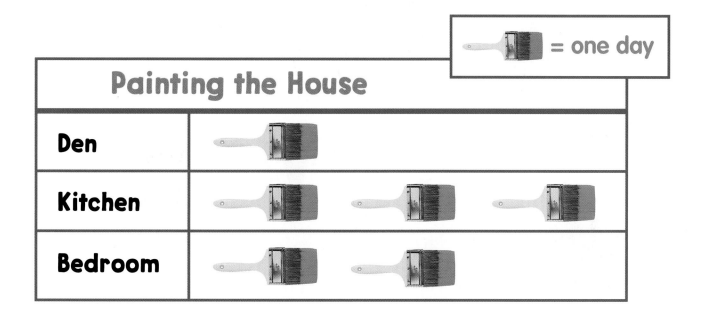

= one day

Painting the House

Den	
Kitchen	
Bedroom	

Try The Skill

1. What does the paintbrush symbol stand for?

2. How many days does it take to paint the bedroom?

 Make a picture graph. Show the number of pictures on each wall of your classroom.

Getting Goods and Services

Most people cannot make or grow all the goods they use. Instead they use money to buy goods from a store.

People also use money to pay for services. Sometimes people buy goods and services and promise to pay for them later.

 Why do most people buy goods?

Trade

You can also **trade** for goods and services. You trade when you give something to get something in return.

These children are trading for toys.

Most people trade work for money. Look at this picture graph. It shows the work Jill does and the money she gets.

Using Picture Graphs

= one dollar

Jill's Jobs

Babysit	💵 💵 💵 💵 💵
Mow Lawn	💵 💵 💵 💵 💵 💵
Walk Dog	💵 💵 💵

Picture Graph Skill

How much money does Jill make when she walks a dog?

Think and Write!

1 How do most people get the goods they need?

2 Name something that you have traded.

Biography

Cesar Chavez

When Cesar Chavez was young, he and his family were farm workers. They were not paid much money.

When Cesar Chavez grew up, he helped begin a group. They called themselves the United Farm Workers. Soon farm workers were paid more money. They were given services that made their lives better.

Explore the life of Cesar Chavez at our Web site www.mhschool.com

Citizenship

Making Decisions
Being Fair

Cesar Chavez tried to be fair. We should try to be fair, too. Look at these pictures. What decision would you make?

I want this cookie.

I want it, too.

Be a Good Citizen

Why is it important to be fair? Ask a parent, teacher, or other adult.

Activity

Draw a picture of a time when someone was fair. Draw a picture of a time when someone was unfair.

5

New Tools at Work

Many people use tools. Tools help them do a better job. Tools have changed over the years.

200

Long ago, farmers used a horse and plow. The horse and plow helped them to plant.

Today farmers use new tools. Now farmers can do more work.

 How do tools help people who work?

Computers at Work

Many years ago, computers were very big. They took up a whole room.

Today computers are smaller. Some computers are so small you can hold them in your hand.

Computers help people work faster. They also help people do more. Computers help people make videos.

How does the computer help workers?

Think and Write!

1 How has the computer changed?

2 How do tools help you?

Putting Things in Order

You put things in **order** when you tell what comes first, next, and last. This is called putting things in order by time.

Look at the pictures. The first picture shows a clown blowing up a balloon. The next picture shows the clown making something with the balloon. What does the last picture show?

Try The Skill

1. Look at these pictures. Put them in order.

2. What story do the pictures tell?

3. Why is it important to put things in order?

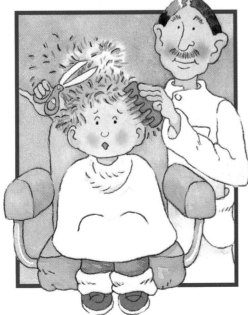

6

People with Great Ideas

People with great ideas help make our work and lives better. You will read about three of these people.

George Washington Carver grew up on a farm. He thought of 100 ways to use the peanut.

 What idea did George Washington Carver have?

More Great Ideas

Many years ago, Alexander Graham Bell had an idea. He made the first telephone.

Ellen Ochoa made a tool that
helps robot arms move in space.
She later became an astronaut.
She worked hard in school.
Read what she wrote.

In her own words

**"If you stay in school,
you have the potential to
achieve what you want."**
—*Ellen Ochoa*

  What did Ellen Ochoa make?

Think and Write!

1. **Why are great ideas important?**

2. **What are some of your ideas?**

A Look at Jobs in Brazil

Brazil is a large country on the continent of South America. People have many kinds of jobs there.

Some people are farmers. They grow coffee, sugarcane, corn, and oranges.

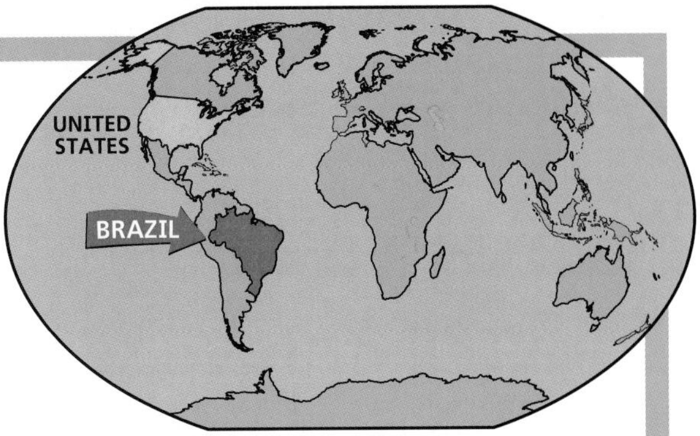

Some people work in the city. São Paulo is the largest city in Brazil. Workers there build goods like computers, cars, and airplanes.

São Paulo

Talk about it!

What kinds of goods do people make in Brazil?

211

Words to Know

Tell if these sentences are true or false. If the sentence is false, tell how to make it true.

1. Work is a job that someone does.

2. A place where people live is called a shelter.

3. Most people do not need goods or services.

Check Your Reading

4. What is an important service job?

5. Why do we need food, clothing, and shelter?

6. Why do we have to choose what we want?

● Using Picture Graphs

7. How many pairs of shoes were sold on Tuesday?

8. How many pairs of shoes were sold all together?

 = one pair of shoes

Shoes Sold in Three Days

Monday	
Tuesday	
Wednesday	

 Make a picture graph. Show the number of crayons or pencils at your desk. Show the number at a friend's desk.

Putting Things in Order

9. What picture should come first?

10. What picture should come last?

Activity

Make a Goods and Services Book

* Draw pictures of goods that you eat or use.

* Draw pictures of services that you use.

* Staple the pages together. Make a cover for your book.

Think and Write

Why do people work?

To learn more about this unit, visit our Web site at **www.mhschool.com**

My Grandma and Me

by Nicole O'Neill

illustrated by Ed Martinez

Kate asked, "What did you do when you were a girl?"

Grandma said, "Let me show you."

216

Grandma said, "I used this to write when I was your age."

Kate said, "It is different from our computer."

"I played records when I was your age," said Grandma.

"I like this music," said Kate.

Grandma said, "I liked to spend time with my Grandma when I was your age. She told me about the past."

Kate said, "I like spending time with you, too."

Talk about it!

Who tells you about the past?

Americans Long Ago

Take a LOOK

These people built new homes in America long ago. What do you know about the past?

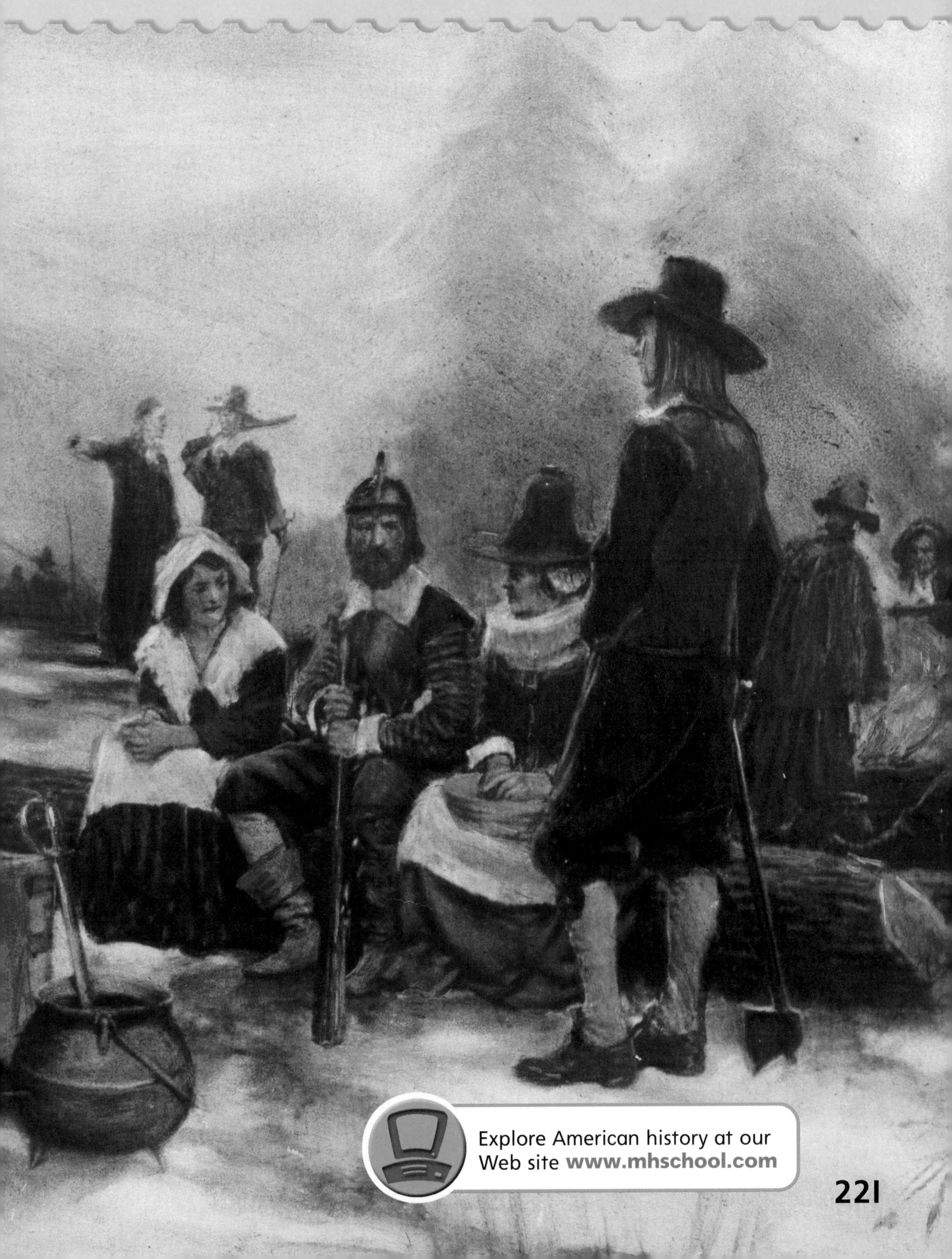

Explore American history at our Web site **www.mhschool.com**

What is History?

History is the story of the past. Read how Carlos learns about the people in his past.

"I look at pictures from the past."

Vietnam Veterans Memorial

"I visit special places."

"I hear stories about the past."

Many people are a part of our country's history. In this unit you will meet some of them.

Words to Know

About History

Find the pictures and say the words.

settlement

Native Americans

settlers

Talk about it!

What do you see in this picture?

Native Americans
Then and Now

Words to Know

Native Americans

226

The first people to live in America were **Native Americans**. Native Americans are also called Indians.

These Native Americans are Apache. In this lesson you will learn about two more groups of Native Americans.

 What is another name for Native Americans?

The Navajo

A long time ago, the Navajo lived on a dry plain. They built homes made of logs and clay. These homes are called "hogans." The Navajo made rugs using yarn.

hogan

Sandra is a Navajo. She lives in New Mexico. She learns how to make rugs from her mother.

NEW MEXICO

 What does Sandra do that the Navajo did long ago?

The Seminole

Long ago the Seminole lived near lakes. They built homes called "chikees." The Seminole played a game we call lacrosse.

lacrosse stick

chikee

FLORIDA

Today the Seminole play games from the past. Tom plays lacrosse. He lives in Florida.

 Why do you think some Seminole play lacrosse?

Think and Write!

1. In what state do some of the Navajo live today?

2. How are the Native Americans in this lesson alike and different?

231

Using Time Lines

A **time line** is a line that shows the order of when things happen.

Rosa made this time line to show her history. Each box stands for one year.

Rosa's Time Line

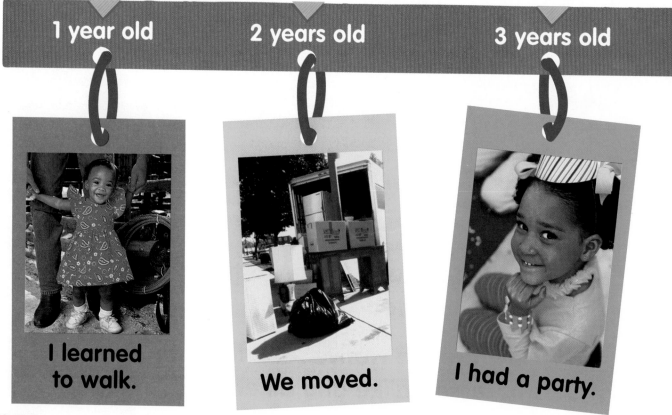

| 1 year old | 2 years old | 3 years old |

I learned to walk.

We moved.

I had a party.

232

Point to the first box. It shows that Rosa learned to walk when she was one year old.

Try The Skill

1. What happened when Rosa was 4?

2. When did Rosa start school?

Make It! Make your own time line.

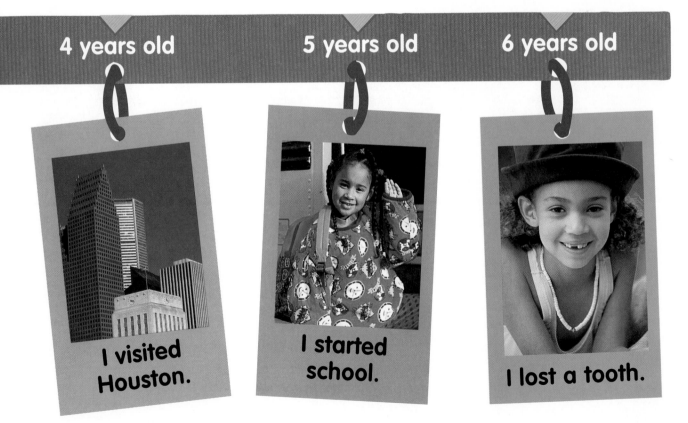

| 4 years old | 5 years old | 6 years old |

I visited Houston.

I started school.

I lost a tooth.

Lesson 2

New People Come to America

Words to Know

settlers
settlement
Pilgrims

Long ago, a group of Native Americans lived on some islands near North America. They were the Taino.

In 1492 Christopher Columbus sailed from Spain. He and his men landed on a Taino island. The Taino and Columbus traded goods.

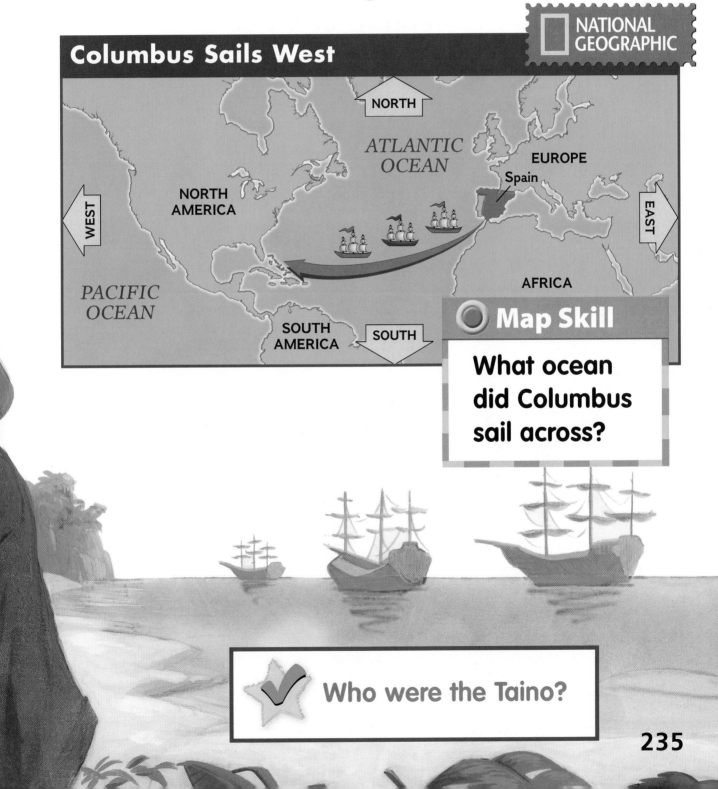

Columbus Sails West

NATIONAL GEOGRAPHIC

NORTH

ATLANTIC OCEAN

EUROPE
Spain

WEST

NORTH AMERICA

EAST

PACIFIC OCEAN

AFRICA

SOUTH AMERICA

SOUTH

○ **Map Skill**

What ocean did Columbus sail across?

✓ **Who were the Taino?**

Settlers

People from many countries came to North America after Columbus. We call these people **settlers**. Settlers are people who move from one place to live in another place.

Settlers from Spain moved north from Mexico. They started new **settlements**. A settlement is a small community. One settlement became Santa Fe, New Mexico.

✓ **Who are settlers?**

The Pilgrims

Later, settlers from England came to North America. They were called the **Pilgrims**. They came for a better life.

The Pilgrims met Native Americans. The Native Americans showed the Pilgrims how to grow food. Soon the Pilgrims had enough food. They celebrated with a special Thanksgiving meal.

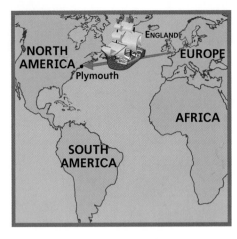

 Why did the Pilgrims come to North America?

Think and Write! ✏️

1. **Who began a settlement in Santa Fe, New Mexico?**

2. **How did the Native Americans help the Pilgrims?**

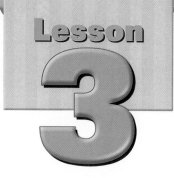

Lesson 3

George Washington

Words to Know

hero

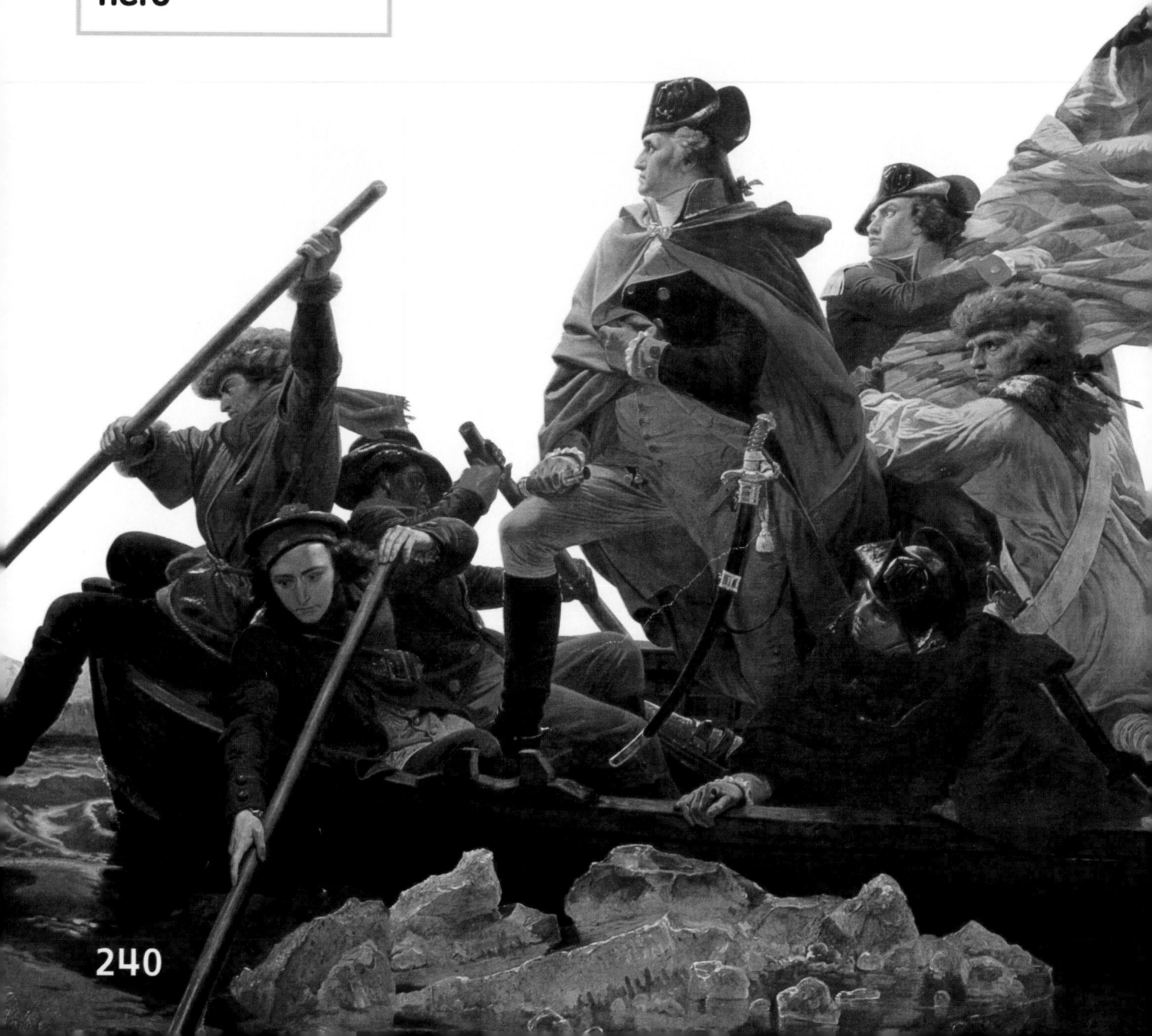

George Washington was born long ago on a farm in Virginia. At that time a country called England ruled America.

America had to follow England's laws. The American people did not like this. They wanted to be free. They went to war with England. They asked George to lead the army.

Why did America want to be free?

Washington Crossing the Delaware

The First President

George Washington helped Americans win the war. America became a country called the United States of America.

George Washington was a **hero** . A hero is a person who does something brave. The people of America made George our first President. He is called the "Father of Our Country."

 How did George Washington become President?

 Think and Write!

1 Why is George called the "Father of Our Country"?

2 How did George Washington help our country?

Sacajawea

Sacajawea lived many years ago. She was a Shoshoni Indian. She helped two men named Lewis and Clark. They wanted to learn more about America.

Sacajawea knew some of the trails to take. She helped Lewis and Clark find a way to the Pacific Ocean.

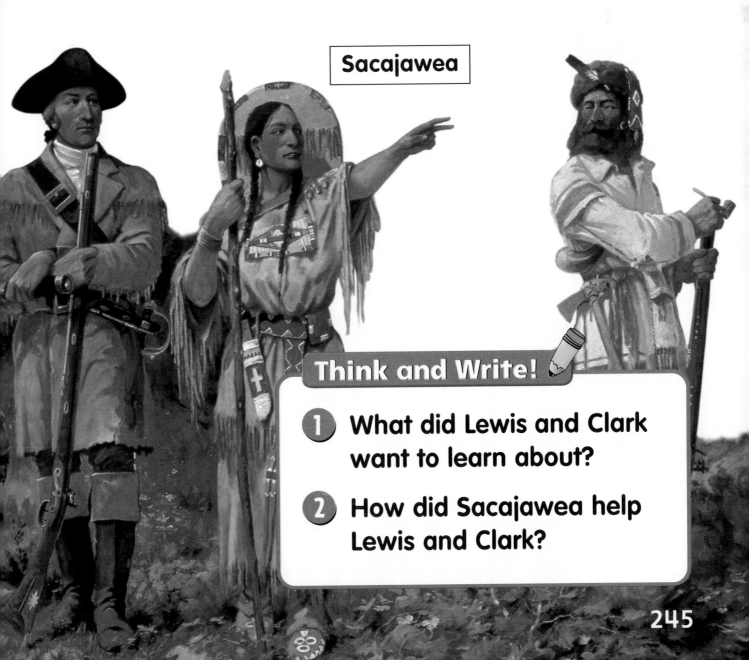

Sacajawea

Think and Write!

1 What did Lewis and Clark want to learn about?

2 How did Sacajawea help Lewis and Clark?

Biography

Sam Houston

Sam Houston is a hero in Texas. Many years ago, Texas was part of Mexico. Sam Houston helped Texas become free.

Sam Houston was the leader of the Texas army. He and his men said, "Remember the Alamo!" Many people had died there. Later, Sam Houston became the governor of Texas.

The Alamo

Explore the life of Sam Houston at our Web site www.mhschool.com

Abraham Lincoln

Abraham Lincoln was born in a log house. Abraham, or Abe, loved to read.

One day, Abe bought something at the store. Later, he saw that he was given too much change. Abe walked to the store and gave the money back. He became known as "Honest Abe."

Where was Abraham Lincoln born?

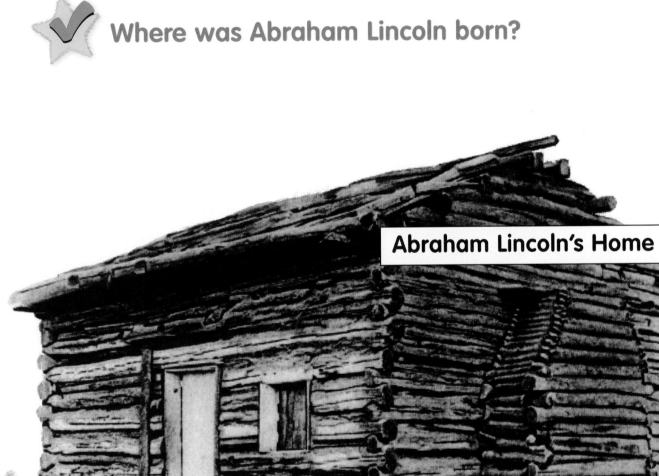

Abraham Lincoln's Home

A Great President

Abraham Lincoln became President of the United States. He was one of our greatest Presidents. Abe helped keep our country together during the Civil War. He also helped slaves become free.

 How did Abraham Lincoln help our country?

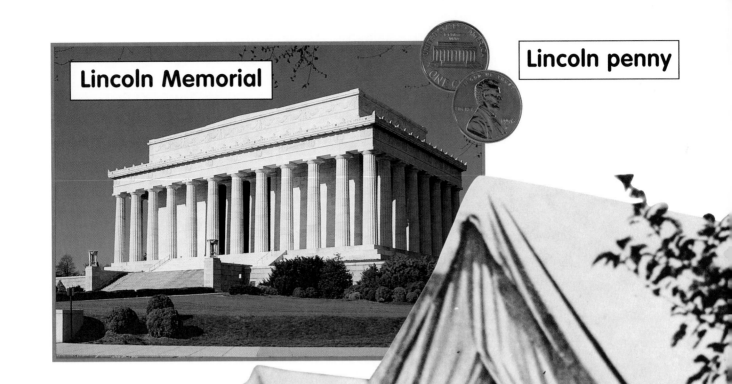

Lincoln Memorial

Lincoln penny

Lincoln with army

Think and Write!

1. Why was Abraham Lincoln called "Honest Abe"?

2. Why was Abraham Lincoln one of our greatest Presidents?

251

Lesson 6

Susan B. Anthony

Long ago, women could not vote. They had to stay at home. Susan B. Anthony knew this was not fair.

Susan B. Anthony worked hard to change things. She wanted women to be able to vote. She was a leader. She talked to many people.

Susan B. Anthony

How were things different for women long ago?

Working for Change

Susan B. Anthony was not alone. Many other women worked to change things. They also wanted to be able to vote.

VOTES FOR US
WHEN
E ARE WOMEN

After many years of work, the
law was changed. Women got
the right to vote!

 Who helped women
become able to vote?

Think and Write!

1. Why is Susan B. Anthony important?

2. Why should all people be able to vote?

Finding the Main Idea

The **main idea** tells what a story is about. It helps you to understand what you read.

Read this story to find the main idea.

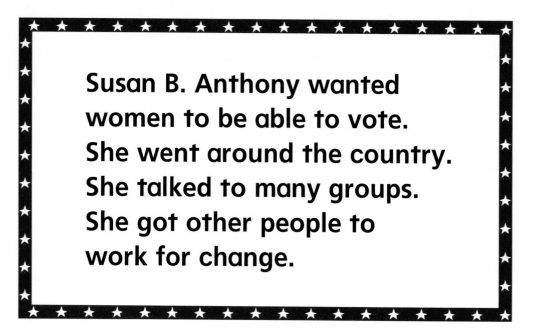

Susan B. Anthony wanted women to be able to vote. She went around the country. She talked to many groups. She got other people to work for change.

Sometimes the main idea of a story is the first sentence. The main idea of this story is that Susan B. Anthony wanted women to be able to vote.

Read this story to find the main idea.

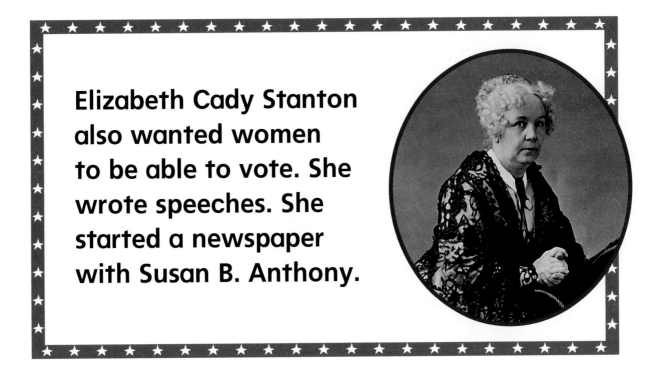

Elizabeth Cady Stanton also wanted women to be able to vote. She wrote speeches. She started a newspaper with Susan B. Anthony.

Try The Skill

1. Which sentence tells the main idea of this story?

2. How can knowing the main idea be helpful?

Celebrate History
with a Poem

Veterans Day with Grandpa

by Bobbi Katz

I'm glad when there's a holiday;
No school, no work, more time to play!
But what is Veterans Day about?
My grandpa helped me to find out.

He opened an old snapshot book.
"What makes a veteran? Take a look.
That was what I used to be."
A snapshot soldier smiled at me.

Now I know that Veterans Day
Is our special chance to say
"Thanks" to those men and
    women who
Gave their best for the red,
    white, and blue.

Martin Luther King, Jr.

Martin Luther King, Jr., grew up in Atlanta, Georgia. At that time black and white children went to different schools. It was the law. Martin knew this law was not fair.

When Martin grew up, he worked to change things. He became a leader. He led marches that asked for fair laws. He wanted to bring people together.

How were things different when Martin was growing up?

Martin's Dream

Martin spoke to many people. He had a dream that all people could work together. His work helped end laws that kept people apart. He is a hero.

Read what Martin Luther King, Jr., said.

In his own words

"We cannot walk alone. And as we walk, we must make the pledge that we shall march ahead. We cannot turn back."

— *Martin Luther King, Jr.*

What was Martin's dream?

Think and Write!

1. How did Martin Luther King, Jr., work for change?

2. Why is Martin Luther King, Jr., a hero?

263

Being a Good Citizen
Ask a Friend

Mrs. Ramsey's class is in Morrisville, North Carolina. There are many helpers in her class. Mrs. Ramsey always says, "Before you come to me, ask a friend for help."

Vuong Le

Chamara Fernando

264

Morrisville, NORTH CAROLINA

Jill Goodtree

Jill Goodtree likes to help with reading. She says, "I help people figure out what a word means or how to say it."

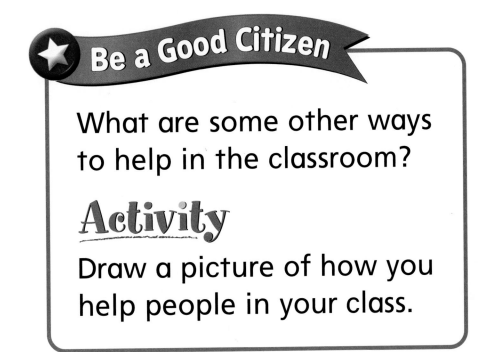

⭐ Be a Good Citizen

What are some other ways to help in the classroom?

Activity

Draw a picture of how you help people in your class.

A Look at
A Hero from Mexico

Miguel Hidalgo is a hero in Mexico. Long ago, Mexico was a part of Spain. Hidalgo helped Mexico become free. He said, "Viva Mexico!" That means, "Long Live Mexico!"

Every year, Mexico remembers Hidalgo. They ring a bell. They celebrate their freedom with a party.

Talk about it!

Why is Miguel Hidalgo remembered each year?

MEXICAN INDEPENDENCE
1810   1960

4¢ JOINT ISSUE MEXICO-UNITED STATES
U.S. POSTAGE

Words to Know

Use these words to finish the sentences.

Native Americans	history	settlement

1. Settlers from Spain built a ____ called Santa Fe.

2. ____ helped the Pilgrims grow food.

3. ____ is the story of our past.

Check Your Reading

4. Who were the first people to live in America?

5. How were Susan B. Anthony and Martin Luther King, Jr., alike?

6. How did George Washington and Abe Lincoln help our country?

Using Time Lines

Matt's Time Line

| Spring | Summer | Fall | Winter |

7. During what season does Matt go ice skating?

8. What does Matt like to do in the summer?

 Make a time line. Show things you do in the spring, summer, winter, and fall.

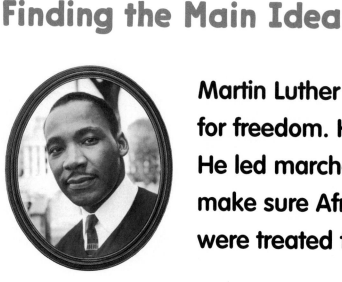

Finding the Main Idea

TEST PREP

Martin Luther King, Jr. worked for freedom. He gave speeches. He led marches. He worked to make sure African Americans were treated fairly.

9. What is the main idea of this story?

- ⬭ Martin led marches.
- ⬭ Martin worked for freedom.
- ⬭ Martin gave speeches.

10. Why is it important to know the main idea?

- ⬭ It helps me understand what I read.
- ⬭ It helps me learn to spell.
- ⬭ It helps me do math problems.

Unit Activity

Make a History Time Line

- ❋ Draw pictures of three things that happened in this unit.

- ❋ Write a sentence about each.

- ❋ Punch a hole in each picture.

- ❋ Hang your pictures on a piece of string.

The Pilgrims came to America.

Think and Write

Why is it important to learn about the past?

To learn more about this unit, visit our Web site at **www.mhschool.com**

Celebrate Holidays

We celebrate many special holidays during the year. Keep reading to learn more about some of them.

Labor Day

We celebrate Labor Day on the first Monday of September. It is the day we celebrate workers. Some families have picnics. It is a day to rest and have fun.

Activity Create a Poster

* Cut out pictures of workers.
* Paste them on paper.
* Label your pictures.

Fireman

Doctor

Teacher

Chef

Thanksgiving

Many years ago, the Pilgrims gave thanks. They celebrated their first Thanksgiving. They had a special meal. They shared it with their friends, the Native Americans.

Today we celebrate Thanksgiving like the Pilgrims. We have a special meal with friends and family. We are thankful for everything we have.

Activity Make a Collage

* Draw pictures of things you are thankful for.
* Paste your pictures on a paper plate turkey.

Special Days

On **Christmas,** Christians celebrate the birth of Jesus. Many of them put stars on top of Christmas trees.

Jewish people celebrate **Hanukkah.** They light candles for 8 nights. Hanukkah is also called the festival of lights.

Some African Americans celebrate **Kwanzaa.** Together they celebrate their past and share food.

Eid al Fitr is the last day of a month called Ramadan. Muslims celebrate with new clothes and food.

Activity Make a Holiday Banner

* Fold your paper in half.
* Write the name of the holiday.
* Draw pictures about the holiday.
* Hang your pictures on string.

Presidents' Day

In February, we celebrate Presidents' Day. This special day helps us remember George Washington and Abraham Lincoln.

Activity   Make a Mobile

* Draw Abraham Lincoln on a circle.
* Write what he did on the back.
* Do the same for George Washington.
* Write Presidents' Day on a circle.
* Put your circles on a hanger.

Presidents' Day

George Washington was the first President of the U.S.

Martin Luther King, Jr., Day

We celebrate Martin Luther King, Jr., Day in January. We remember the work of Martin Luther King, Jr., on this day. We remember how his work made America a better place.

Activity   Make a Class Friendship Circle

* Trace a friend's hand. Cut out the shape.
* Write a sentence about being friends.
* Paste the hands in a big circle. Add the sentences.

Friendship Circle

Any person can be a friend.

Let's all be friends.

People should work together.

Be nice to your neighbor.

Be kind to all people.

Cinco de Mayo

Cinco de Mayo means the "5th of May" in Spanish. It celebrates the battle Mexico won over France many years ago. Today, Mexican Americans celebrate with parties and parades.

Activity Make a Poncho

* Cut a hole in a paper bag for your head.
* Cut a slit on each side for your arms.
* Paint designs on the bag.
* Add bits of fabric and yarn with glue.

Flag Day

We celebrate Flag Day on June 14. On that day long ago, our country chose its first flag. To celebrate, we fly the American flag.

Activity Make a Card

* Fold a sheet of paper in half.
* Draw a picture of our flag on the outside.
* Write a Flag Day message on the inside.

Independence Day

Independence Day celebrates the birth of the United States of America. It is also called the Fourth of July. We celebrate with parades. We also celebrate with fireworks.

Long Ago

Today

Activity Make a Star

* Trace a star on a piece of paper. Cut it out.
* Decorate your star with glitter and crayons.
* Glue streamers to the bottom of the star.

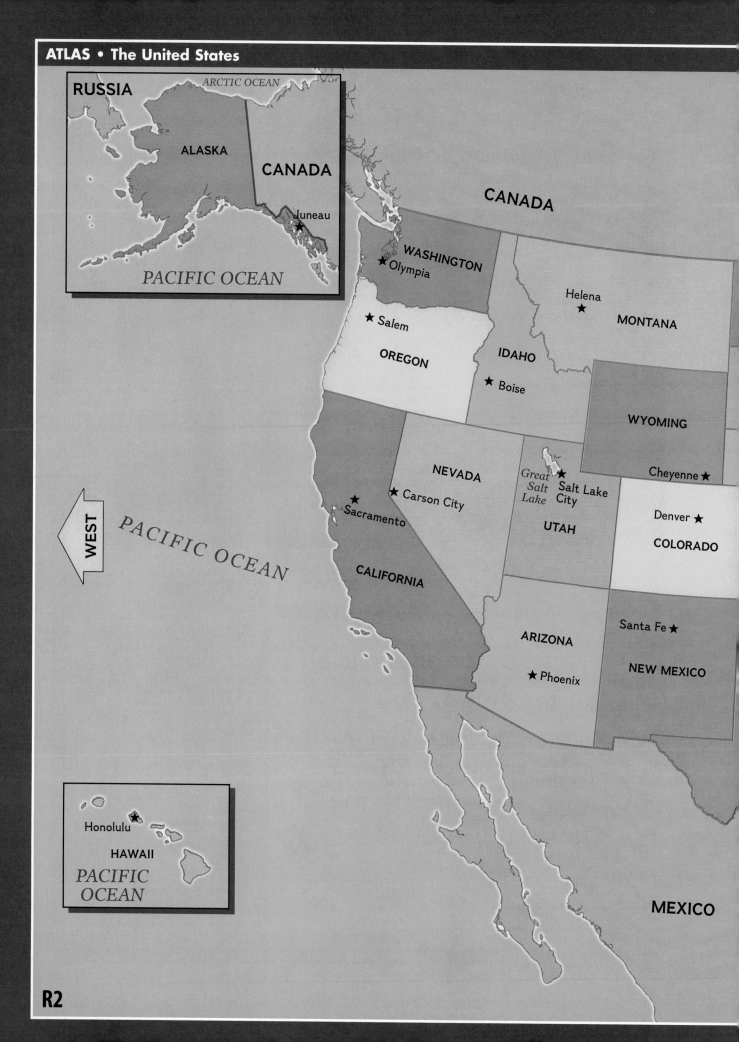

RUSSIA

ARCTIC OCEAN

ALASKA

CANADA

★Juneau

PACIFIC OCEAN

CANADA

WASHINGTON
★ Olympia

Helena
★
MONTANA

★ Salem

OREGON

IDAHO

★ Boise

WYOMING

WEST

PACIFIC OCEAN

NEVADA

★ Carson City

Great Salt Lake ★ Salt Lake City

Cheyenne ★

Denver ★

COLORADO

★ Sacramento

UTAH

CALIFORNIA

Santa Fe ★

ARIZONA

★ Phoenix

NEW MEXICO

Honolulu ★

HAWAII

PACIFIC OCEAN

MEXICO

NORTH

CANADA

MAINE
Augusta

VERMONT
NEW
HAMPSHIRE
Montpelier
Concord
MASSACHUSETTS
Albany
Boston
NEW
YORK
Providence
Hartford
CONNECTICUT
RHODE
ISLAND

NORTH
DAKOTA
Bismarck

MINNESOTA

Lake Superior

Lake Huron

MICHIGAN

Lake Michigan

Lake Ontario

Lake Erie

SOUTH
DAKOTA
Pierre

St. Paul

WISCONSIN

Madison

Lansing

PENNSYLVANIA
Harrisburg

Trenton
NEW JERSEY
Dover
DELAWARE

NEBRASKA

IOWA
Des
Moines

ILLINOIS

Indianapolis

OHIO

Columbus

Washington,
D.C.
Annapolis
MARYLAND

EAST

Lincoln

Springfield

INDIANA

WEST
VIRGINIA
Charleston
Richmond
VIRGINIA

Topeka

KANSAS

MISSOURI
Jefferson
City

Frankfort

KENTUCKY

NORTH
CAROLINA
Raleigh

Nashville

OKLAHOMA
Oklahoma
City

ARKANSAS

TENNESSEE

ATLANTIC
OCEAN

SOUTH
Columbia
CAROLINA

Little
Rock

MISSISSIPPI

Atlanta

ALABAMA

GEORGIA

Jackson

TEXAS

LOUISIANA

Montgomery

Tallahassee

Baton
Rouge

FLORIDA

Austin

THE
BAHAMAS

Gulf of Mexico

National capital   State capital

CUBA

SOUTH

R3

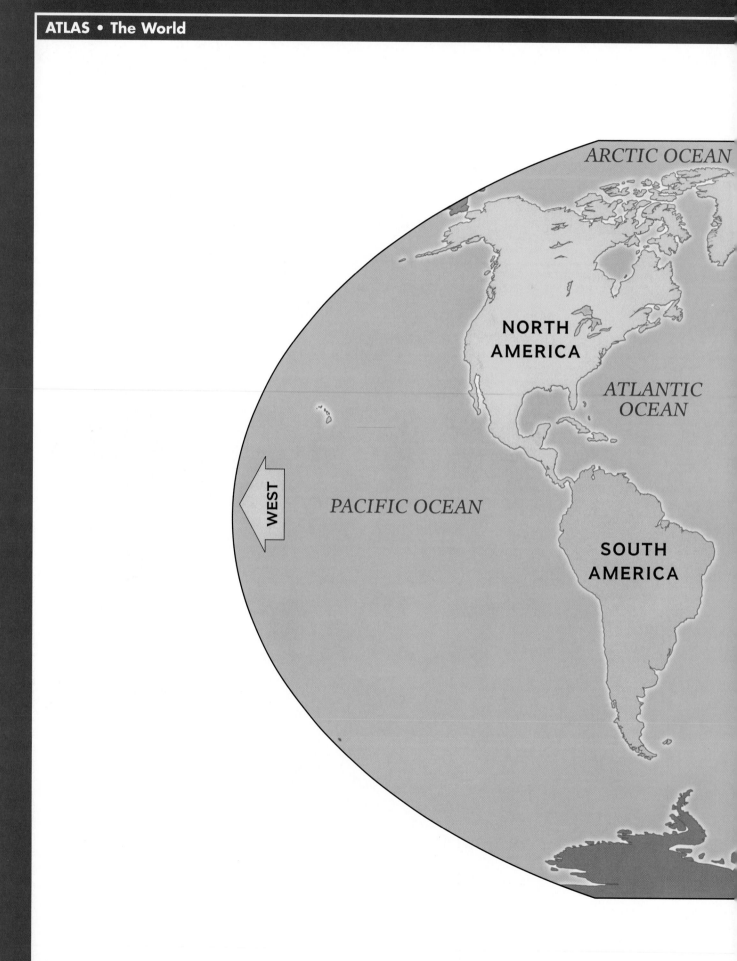

ARCTIC OCEAN

NORTH
AMERICA

ATLANTIC
OCEAN

WEST

PACIFIC OCEAN

SOUTH
AMERICA

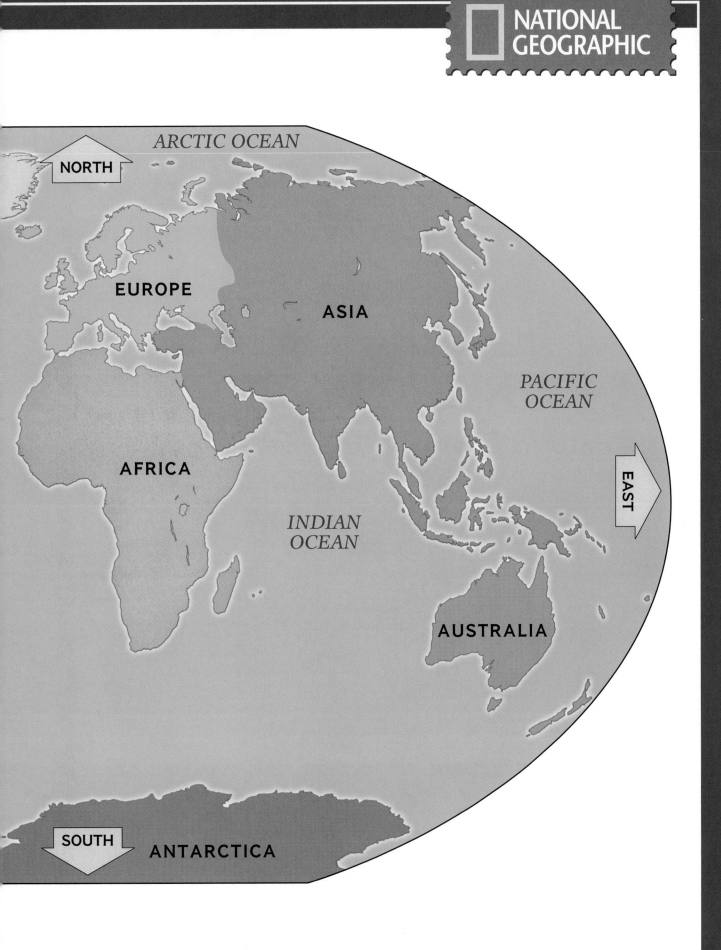

NATIONAL GEOGRAPHIC

ARCTIC OCEAN

NORTH

EUROPE

ASIA

PACIFIC OCEAN

AFRICA

EAST

INDIAN OCEAN

AUSTRALIA

SOUTH ANTARCTICA

Dictionary of Geographic Words

HILL—Land that is higher than the land around it, but lower than a mountain.

LAKE—Body of water with land all around it.

PLAIN—Flat land.

MOUNTAIN— Highest kind of land.

RIVER—Long body of water that flows across the land.

OCEAN—Very large body of salt water.

Picture Glossary

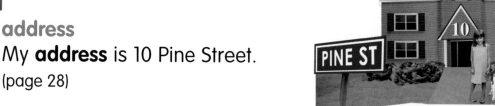

A

address

My **address** is 10 Pine Street.
(page 28)

C

calendar

This **calendar** shows the month of November.
(page 150)

celebrate

I **celebrate** my birthday once a year.
(page 18)

chart

Mike's **chart** shows how he gets places. (page 40)

citizen

I am a **citizen** of the United States of America. (page 120)

city

There are many buildings in my **city**. (page 67)

community

I live in a **community**.

(page 66)

continent

North America is a **continent** on Earth. (page 78)

NORTH AMERICA

country

The United States of America is our **country**. (page 74)

D

directions

North, south, east and west are **directions**. (page 128)

North

West   East

South

E

Earth

We live on the planet **Earth**.

(page H11)

F

factory

A **factory** is a place where goods are made. (page 187)

Picture Glossary

family
Mary has fun with her **family**.
(page 10)

farm
Grandpa grows plants on his **farm**.
(page 70)

flag
The United States **flag** is red, white, and blue. (page 143)

G

geography
Geography tells you where places are and what they are like. (page 62)

globe
A **globe** is a model of Earth. (page H12)

goods
Food and clothing are **goods** you can buy. (page 186)

governor
A **governor** is the leader of a state.
(page 134)

group
People who do things together make a **group**. (page 124)

H

hero
Joe the fire fighter is my **hero**. (page 243)

hill
A **hill** is land higher than the land around it. (page 88)

history
History is what happened in the past. (page 222)

holiday
Kwanzaa is my favorite **holiday**.
(page 20)

Picture Glossary

L

lake
A **lake** is a body of water with land all around it. (page 87)

law
It is the **law** that drivers must stop at a stop sign. (page 130)

leader
This police officer is a **leader** in his community. (page 132)

M

main idea
The **main idea** tells you what a story is about. (page 256)

map
This **map** shows you the state I live in. (page H10)

Alaska

ALASKA

map key
A **map key** tells you what symbols on a map mean. (page 90)

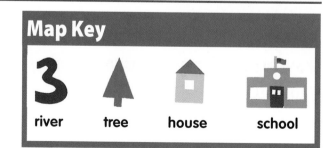

Map Key

river tree house school

mayor
A **mayor** is the leader of a community.
(page 134)

mountain
Mountains are the highest kind of
land. (page 89)

N

Native Americans
The first people to live in America were
Native Americans. (page 227)

natural resource
Water is a **natural resource** that people
and animals need to live. (page 96)

needs
Shelter, food, clothing, and love
are **needs**. (page 176)

neighbor
Joe and Bill are **neighbors**.
(page 68)

Picture Glossary

O

ocean

An **ocean** is a very large body of water. (page 80)

order

I can write my numbers in **order** from 1-10. (page 204)

$$1 \; 2 \; 3 \; 4 \; 5 \; 6 \; 7 \; 8 \; 9 \; 10$$

P

picture graph

This **picture graph** shows how many shoes were sold in three days. (page 190)

Pilgrims

The **Pilgrims** were settlers in North America. (page 238)

plain

A **plain** is a flat piece of land. (page 88)

President

The **President** is the leader of our country. (page 135)

problem

John had a **problem** finding his friend's house. (page 34)

R

river

A **river** flows across the land. (page 87)

rule

It is a **rule** that you must raise your hand. (page 30)

S

season

My favorite **season** is fall. (page 94)

service

The dentist takes care of our teeth. That is a **service**. (page 188)

settlement

The Pilgrims built a **settlement**. (page 237)

Picture Glossary

settlers

People who move from one place to live in another place are called **settlers**. (page 236)

shelter

My house is a **shelter**.
(page 177)

solve

The teacher helped me **solve** my problem. (page 34)

sort

I **sorted** my beads by color.
(page 76)

state

Texas is a **state** in the United States of America. (page 74)

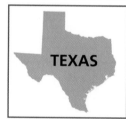

TEXAS

symbol

The Statue of Liberty is a **symbol** of the United States of America. (page 90)

T

time line

Lee made a **time line** of his life. (page 232)

Lee's Time Line

3 years old	5 years old	6 years old
Learns to swim	Starts school	Joins soccer team

trade

I would like to **trade** this toy for that toy. (page 194)

transportation

The bus is my **transportation** to school. (page 37)

V

volunteer

A **volunteer** helps me with my school work. (page 183)

vote

We took a **vote** on what game to play. (page 140)

W

wants

Wants are things we would like to have. (page 178)

weather

The **weather** today is rainy. (page 92)

work

Lisa does her **work** at school. (page 172)

Index

Addresses, using, 28–29, 54
Africa, 51, 81
African Americans, 136–137, 154, 260, 276
Alamo, 247
Alike and different, 17, 25, 27, 39, 52, 71, 73, 76, 89, 94, 108, 157, 161, 187, 230–231
America, 158, 241, 242
Anthony, Susan B., 252–255
Arkansas, 75
Art, 184, 185
Atlanta, Georgia, 260
Asking a friend, 264–265

B

Bald eagle, 146
Barton, Clara, 155
Being fair, 198–199
Bell, Alexander Graham, 208
Bethune, Mary McLeod, 136–137
Brazil, 210, 211
Bush, George W., 135

C

Calendars, using, 150–151, 164
California, 68
Canada, 79
Carson, Rachel, 102–103
Carver, George Washington, 207
Celebrate, 12–13, 18–23, 50–51, 84, 158, 184, 258
Charts, using, 40–41, 45, 53, 93, 126–127
Chavez, Cesar, 196–198
Chicago, Illinois, 67
Chile, 26
China, 26
Choice, making, 178–179
Christmas, 20–21, 276

Cinco de Mayo, 280
Citizens, 48–49, 104–105, 118–119, 120–123, 138–139, 152–157, 162, 199, 264–265
Citizenship, 48–49, 104–105, 112–117, 138–139, 198–199
City, 64–67, 108
Civil War, 250
Clovis, California, 68
Communities, 66–68, 71, 82, 113, 237
Computers, 44–45, 202–203, 211, 217
Continents, 78–81, 83
Country, 74–76, 78–79, 83, 106

D

Days of the week, 2, 6, 7
December, 20–21
Decision making, 198–199
Directions, using, 128–129, 163
Douglass, Frederick, 154–155

Eagle, bald, 146
Earth, 80, 83, 86–89, 103, 128
Economics, 166–215
Edison, Thomas, 46–47
Eid al Fitr, 277
England, 238–239, 241
Europe, 81, 106

F

Factory, 187
Fall, 95
Families, 8–13, 14–17, 18–21, 24–27, 30–33, 36–39, 42–45, 50–55, 60–65, 70, 72, 82
Farms, 64, 66, 70–71

Farmers, 200–201, 210
Flag, American, 122, 142–143, 281
Flag Day, 281
Florida, 231
Fourth of July, 12–13, 150–151, 282–283

Geography, 28–29, 60–65, 72–73, 106–108
using addresses, 28–29
using pictures, maps, globes, 63, 72–73, 128
Getting along, 138–139
Goods, 174, 186–187, 192–194, 211–212
Governor, 134
Greece, 26
Groups, 76–77, 122, 124–125, 162

H

Hale, Nathan, 152–153
Hanukkah, 21, 276
Helpers, 112–117, 264–265
Hero, 243, 263, 266–267
Hidalgo, Miguel, 266–267
Hills, 88
History, 220–221, 268
Holidays, 12, 18–21, 52, 272–283
for country, 12, 20–21, 272–283
for families, 20–21, 52
special days, 272–283
Homes, 24–27, 82, 228, 230
Hong Kong, 26
Houston, Sam, 246–247

I

Idaho, 88
Independence Day, 12–13, 150–151, 282–283
Iowa, 88

Jamuhuri Day, 50
Japan, 160–161
Jobs, 170–173, 180–183, 188–189, 210– 212

K

Kentucky, 99
Kenya, 50–51
King, Jr., Martin Luther, 260–263, 279
Kwanzaa, 20, 276

L

Labor Day, 273
Lake, 87
Land, 87, 89, 100–101
Laws, 130–131
Leaders, 132–137
Lewis and Clark, 244–245
Lewisburg, West Virgina, 70
Liberty Bell, 147
Light bulb, 46–47
Lincoln, Abraham, 248–251, 278
Lincoln Memorial, 251
Literature
    The Ant and the Grasshopper, 166–169
    "A Good Helper," 112–117
    "Hooray for Saturday!," 2–7
    The Legend of Johnny Appleseed, 56–59
    My Grandma and Me, 216–219

M

Main idea, finding the, 256–257, 270
Map keys, using, 90–91, 93, 99, 109

Maps
  Arkansas, 75
  Canada, 79
  Columbus sails west, 235
  Community, 109
  Florida, 231
  Kentucky, 99
  Kenya, Africa, 51
  Mexico, 79, 267
  Morrisville, North
    Carolina, 265
  New Mexico, 229, 237
  Switzerland, 107
  United States and Its
    Neighbors, 79
  Washington, D.C., 135
  World, 80–81
Maps, using, 63, 72–73, 81,
  91, 109, 128, 163
Map symbols, 90–91
Massachusetts, 134
Mayor, 134–135
Messages, sending, 44–45
Mexico, 79, 237, 246,
  266–267
Minnesota, 87
Mississippi River, 87
Missouri, 75
Money, 183, 193, 195, 249
Months of the year, 12,
  20–21, 151, 164, 273, 275,
  276–282
Morocco, 27
Mountains, 64–65, 89, 107
Mount McKinley, 89

Native Americans,
  224–235, 239, 244–245
Natural resources
  caring for, 100–101,
    104–105
  types of, 96–99
Navajo, 228–229
Needs, 176–177, 179

Neighbors, 66, 68–69, 71,
  113
New Mexico, 229
New York Harbor, 148
North America, 78, 79, 81,
  89, 236, 238
North Pole, 128

Oceans, 78, 80, 86, 235
Ochoa, Ellen, 209

Pacific Ocean, 86
People with Great Ideas,
  206–209
Philadelphia,
  Pennsylvania, 147
Pictures, using, 63, 72–73,
  213
Picture graphs, using,
  190–191, 195, 213
Pilgrims, 238–239
Places, 62
Plain, 88
Pledge of Allegiance, 118,
  144–145
Poems
  "A Good Helper,"
    112–117
  "Hooray For Saturday!,"
    2–7
  "Pride," 22–23
  "Veterans Day with
    Grandpa," 259
President, 122, 135, 162,
  242, 243, 250–251, 278
Presidents' Day, 278
Problem solving, 34–35, 54
Putting things in order,
  204–205, 214

Ramadan, 277
Red Cross, 155

River, 64, 86, 87
Roosevelt, Eleanor, 137,
  156–157
Rules, 30–33, 52, 55, 116,
  126–127, 138–139

Sacajawea, 244–245
Santa Fe, New Mexico, 237
São Paulo, Brazil, 211
Seasons, 94–95
Seminole, 230–231
Services, 174, 188, 189,
  192–194, 197, 212
Settlement, 224–225, 237
Settlers, 224–225, 236
Shelter, 174, 177, 212
Songs
  "Big Beautiful Planet,"
    84–85
  "My Country, 'Tis of
    Thee," 158–159
  "Star-Spangled Banner,"
    144
Sorting, 76–77, 110
South America, 81, 210
Spring, 94
Stanton, Elizabeth Cady,
  257
States, 67, 68, 74–75, 82,
  83, 87, 88, 92, 93
Statue of Liberty, 148
Summer, 94
Switzerland, 106–107
Symbol, map, 90–91
Symbols, 142–149

Taino, 234–235
Texas, 246–247
Thanksgiving Day, 164,
  239, 274–275
Time lines, using,
  232–233, 269, 271
Tools, 200–201, 209

Town, 68
Trade, 194–195
Trains, 37
Transportation, 12, 36–41,
  52
Trees, 58, 59, 91, 99

Uncle Sam, 149, 162
United Farm Workers, 197
United States
  flag of, 122, 142–143
  holidays and, 12, 20–21,
    164, 272–283
  neighboring countries, 79
  President, 138, 243, 250,
    278
  symbols of, 142–149, 159

Veterans Day, 259
Volunteers, 183
Voting, 122, 123, 140–141,
  252–255

Wants, 178–179
Washington (state), 92, 93
Washington, D.C., 135
Washington, George, 153,
  240–243, 278
Water, 72–73, 86–87,
  96–97
Weather, 64, 92–95, 108
Winter, 95
Work, 170–175, 180–185,
  188-189, 200–203, 212
World, 78–85, 100–101,
  104–105, 160–161

Credits

Acknowledgments (continued from page ii)

From *Hispanic*, May 1990. **Ellen Ochoa: The First Hispanic Woman Astronaut** by Maritza Romero. Copyright © 1997 PowerKids Press. Used by permission.

"Veterans Day with Grandpa" by Bobbi Katz. Copyright © 2001 by Bobbi Katz. Used by permission.

From "I Have a Dream" from **A Call to Conscience: The Landmark Speeches of Dr. Martin Luther King, Jr.,** Clayborne Carson and Kris Shepard, eds. IPM/Warner Books, 2001. Copyright © The Estate of Martin Luther King, Jr. Used by permission.